T0157843

Son of (Entropy)²

Personal Memories of a Son of a Chemist, Joseph E. Mayer, and a
Nobel Prize Winning Physicist, Maria Goeppert Mayer

Peter C. Mayer

authorHOUSE®

AuthorHouse™
1663 Liberty Drive
Bloomington, IN 47403
www.authorhouse.com
Phone: 1-800-839-8640

© 2011.Peter C. Mayer All rights reserved

No part of this book may be reproduced, stored in a retrieval system, or transmitted by any means without the written permission of the author.

First published by AuthorHouse   07/28/2011

ISBN: 978-1-4634-2069-7 (sc)
ISBN: 978-1-4634-2067-3 (e)

Library of Congress Control Number: 2011909237

Printed in the United States of America

This book is printed on acid-free paper.

Because of the dynamic nature of the Internet, any web addresses or links contained in this book may have changed since publication and may no longer be valid. The views expressed in this work are solely those of the author and do not necessarily reflect the views of the publisher, and the publisher hereby disclaims any responsibility for them.

Dedicated to

Maria Anne Wentzel,

Daughter of

(Entropy)^2

"With Daughter"
CREDIT American Instutute of Physics, Emilio Segre Visual Archives

Contents

Introduction, Who Are Entropy and Entropy?

This book is a collection of vignettes, remembered by the son of the human side of two very human people. It is written mostly to be fun. My upbringing was mostly fun. Well, not really. It *contained* a lot of fun and would have been mostly fun if my misbehavior did not require my father's heavy-handed discipline and my mother's usually more subtle discipline. Like most of us, any statement about upbringing being fun must be qualified with "aside from the consequences of my misbehavior."

Most who knew Maria Goeppert Mayer and Joseph E. Mayer agree that their human characteristics equaled their scientific accomplishments, and their science reflected their human characteristics. There is a building with a special seminar room at the University of California at San Diego, both named after my parents. In 1963, my mother was the second woman to earn a Nobel Prize in physics and the third to earn a Nobel Prize in science. My father earned numerous awards, and there is a Joseph E. Mayer Chair of Theoretical Chemistry at the University of California at San Diego. In the first half of his career, Joe performed experimental chemistry as well.

My parents' jointly authored *Statistical Mechanics*—an excellent book. It was published in 1940, and in 1960 and 1961 classmates at Caltech referred to Mayer and Mayer. (My father completed a second edition in 1977.) Entropy is an important concept in thermodynamics, which is the subject of the book. Most physicists and chemists would recognize the reference $(Entropy)^2$ and correctly guess who the Son of $(Entropy)^2$ is. When I changed my field from physics, a classmate found it a pity that there would never be a Mayer, Mayer, and Mayer.

My father was the better scientist. To explain, the Nobel Prize is not awarded for a person's total achievements but for an impressive piece of work. My mother was not very productive, but most of what she authored was of very high quality. Most impressive is that the piece that earned her the Nobel Prize was initially published as a mere note.

Nepotism Prohibitions

A son of a long-term colleague of my parents observed that Maria would have been more productive without nepotism prohibitions preventing her from being paid. Nepotism prohibitions certainly were not welcome; however, their interference with Maria's scientific accomplishments was limited. With top scientists, in addition to my father, appreciating her science, even the patronizing early in her career probably had limited impact. Joe's encouragement and respect were critical. She was usually not paid by the universities where my father served. Nevertheless, these universities provided her the intellectual stimulus of great universities by providing her an office, access to university facilities, particularly faculty seminars, and faculty interaction. These universities received at a low price—at a steal—her instruction and the stimulus she provided. In academic journal articles, included with the article author's name is the institution with which the author is associated. While Johns Hopkins University, Columbia University, and University of Chicago were not paying her, these institutions received the honor of their name being included in her publications.

A comment is in order. The motive for prohibitions against hiring couples had little to do with anti-feminism. At the time of Joe's first job, the Depression resulted in customs and rules to discourage participation in the labor force. Many of these customs and rules remained through the early 1960s.

Her instruction, the stimulus she provided, and the inclusion of the institution's name in her publications became pricier during her last year at the University of Chicago and later at University of California at San Diego. In response to the University of California offer, which included a half-time salary for Maria, University of Chicago gave her a full-time full professorship. A reason, probably the principal reason for Joe and Maria accepting the California offer, was expressed in a letter to me from my mother, in which she said, "It would be nice to garden all year."

How True Are the Stories?

Since my father was definitely not a braggart, the stories he furnished likely understate his positive accomplishments and likely overstate his foolishness. He would annoy me by responding to my corrections of a story with "don't spoil a good story with the truth." In this case, however, he usually did not practice what he preached. My mother was less bombastic than her husband in her story telling and not a braggart.

Corrections and additions from relatives while drafting this collection, however, show that my memory might not be entirely accurate with respect to detail. The sense of the stories, however, is quite accurate.

Chapter 1:

The Beginning, Göttingen Pre-WWII

The Hollisters

My father, while dining in the Göttingen Ratskeller ...

Oh! For those who are unfamiliar with German towns, the translation for *Rathaus* is city hall, but various characteristics give the Rathaus a different meaning. As an example, the Rathaus is usually a grand old building, often only second in grandeur to the cathedral. Usually, the Rathaus cellar contains the *Ratskeller*, a quality restaurant, often the best in town. Joe spent enough time in the Ratskeller to acquire a favorite waiter. As late as 1950, Joe had this waiter serve us.

While dining in the Göttingen Ratskeller, my father noticed an American couple enjoying themselves and speaking German. (My mother would correct the story with, "you said 'a California couple.'" Dad tended to avoid Americans; they interfered with his goal of learning German, and he didn't like chronic complainers. He approached the couple and was given ice cold shoulders. His thoughts: "What a nice looking couple, but they are most unpleasant," or something less kind. Later, the couple, Joe and Kay Hollister, approached my father and asked him to join them. They, too, did not like chronic complainers.

Kay would party with her husband and Joe in bars where no respectable German lady would go. My mother said she would never have gone to these bars. Kay would walk home, sometimes singing and at times with a Joe on each arm.

Later, while my father was introducing my mother to the American West, they wrote every Hollister in the Santa Barbara phone book. Each put their letter in Joe Hollister's box at the Hollister Estate Company—a pretentious name for Hollister Ranch—office. My parents received a letter from Kay that included the instruction to stop at the Gaviota Store for directions on how to get to the ranch house. At the Gaviota Store, the response to the request for instructions to the Hollister Ranch was, "You came from the North? You have been on the ranch for the last one hundred miles."

There were several exchanges similar to, "We would like to have instructions to go the ranch house."

"Why do you want to go to the ranch house? It is on a long, narrow, difficult dirt road. Besides, the road is private."

In exasperation, my father said, "We were told by Joe and Kay Hollister to ask you for instructions."

"Oh yes," the store owner said, taking a deep breath, "Mrs. Kay told me about you."

Later, when showing their children the American West, my parents often stopped to see the Hollisters. As children, both my sister and I liked the couple, and as an adult I would often visit the widow, Kay. While in high school, I worked one summer for Joe Hollister's brother on the Ranch and two years, while in college, I spent Thanksgiving with his brother.

A tale about the lad, Joe Hollister, was the major component of a Joe Mayer this-is-the-way-to-behave lecture.

"When Joe Hollister was about your age, he walked through an open gate that was usually kept closed. He decided to close the gate. Later, his father and other cowboys tried to drive a herd of cattle through the closed gate."

As a lad, I required that the instructional point be explained, "Leave things, in particular doors and gates, the way you found them."

My Father, That American

I was dating the daughter of a fellow student of Maria's at the University of Göttingen. The first thing the daughter said to me after Christmas vacation was "I know who you are!"

"What do you know about me that you did not know before?"
"Well, I know who your father is!"
"Okay Nickie, what's the story?"

"My father said, 'There were few women students at the University of Göttingen and only one really feminine student. That American,'" Joe Mayer, "'came and purchased a car and took her away.'" At one point, she suggested that it was a sports car. I corrected her. The car was an Opal—at the time the cheapest German car—with a bad clutch. As a postdoctoral fellow, my father had a little more money than the graduate students, but more significantly, he had more gumption.

Later Nickie said, "My father said, 'Be sure to tell Maria's son that Joe had an American directness that charmed all of us.'"

Background

Being feminine results from my mother's upbringing. Some biographies credit my grandfather with telling Maria, "I do not want you to be a woman." This claim is garbage. He said, "I want you to be more than a woman." Too many university women at my mother's time chose not to be women, as was often the case among science and engineering majors even a generation and more later.

My grandfather was a pediatrician. To show that he wanted Maria to also be a woman, he had her attend his lectures on child rearing. Further, all his female patients, including my mother, were vaccinated for small pox high on the thigh so the ugly scar—at that time three scars—would not be visible when wearing sleeveless dresses. Surely, he wished—but did not expect—all his female patients to have interests outside the house as well.

For readers who have not had a small pox vaccination, you might ask an older person to show you their now faded vaccination scar. A small pox vaccination is usually given on the outside of the arm below the shoulder. To vaccinate for small pox, one puts a viscous liquid containing the cowpox virus on the skin. Then the inoculator takes a pin or needle and makes numerous pricks or small cuts within a circle under the liquid. The pricks and the reaction leave a nasty pox as a scar. To minimize total scarring, revaccinations were made on top of the old scar. Among most people alive today, the vaccination left a single scar the size of a dime (US ten-cent piece). However, in earlier times the pinpricks were done within three circles, leaving an unattractive triangle of three scars, each about the size of a nickel (a US five-cent piece). Having seen such a triangle of scares on a Palauan lovely, I know they stand out. Palau was a Japanese trust until the end of World War II and Japanese still made a triangle of scars with small pox vaccinations.

Maria's Influence on Men

Confirming Maria's fellow student's observation, a friend of my father's from graduate school told me the following. "I saw Joe with your mother when she was pregnant with one of you (I have a sister). As I approached them, she looked like a German hausfrau, not at all the kind of woman Joe would marry. At a later time, I saw Joe with a lovely woman and wondered if Joe had a mistress. As I approached, Joe said, 'I believe you have met my wife,' and Maria said, 'Oh yes, we have met.'"

A biographer credits my sister as saying men were putty under my mother's influence. I believe my sister would agree that the limits of language make this assessment an understatement. After all, she witnessed, more often than I did, my mother (or a driver in a car in which my mother was riding) being let go by a policeman intending to issue a traffic citation. I never claim that observing my mother's ability to mold men has made me immune to feminine manipulation, but I will claim that, unlike most men, it never happens without my knowing it.

Women have reported that men would gravitate towards my mother whenever she entered the room. I never noticed, perhaps due to my own gravitation.

There was a very rude visiting professor at the University of

Chicago who eventually was rude to my mother. My mother's reaction was to be glad to be included among those to whom he was rude. At least some of the male professors' reaction was special anger with his behavior towards my mother because he acted his rude way to a woman, spoken in a tone I would use for a woman I found womanly.

Small Tales

Meeting the Awful Flirt

A biographer credits my father when meeting Maria as finding her an awful flirt. An observation from my mother's side may explain why. After meeting Joe asking to board at her mother's house, Maria told her mother, "He is an American." The response was, "Is he like Stanley?" (a former American boarder who recommended that Joe inquire about boarding at the Göppert's). "Yes, but I believe he is much nicer.

Remember Middle School Humor and Watch Your Language

One evening, Joe fully cooperated with a competitor for Maria insisting on speaking English. When arguing who would take Maria home, the competitor agreed to my father's proposition of "heads I win, tails you lose." Mother seemed to enjoy the antics. I am unsure if she fully understood the bet Joe proposed".

If You Hiccup …

"Maria, if you hiccup one more time, I will give you a pineapple!"

My mother really enjoyed even unripe pineapples. (Until at least 1955, the pineapples that shipped as fresh were those rejected for canning because they were not yet ripe.) Having already bought the pineapple, Joe gave it to her even though Maria failed to perform the act. I hope that at least once in her life she had a pineapple as good as the local one that reminded me of this story. As children, neither my sister nor I received the nickel (US five cent piece) offered for hiccupping one more time.

The Opal

The Opal was an automobile, not a gem, although it may have been a gem for courting. It had a bad, noisy clutch. In the Opal, on the back roads around Göttingen, my father taught my mother how to drive. *"Auch,* Maria, you have to have the right relaxed attitude. Have a cigarette." She let the cigarette burn until she had burns between her fingers.

At the time in Germany, the driving test not only included driving around and parallel parking but also backing around a town square and knowledge of the workings of a car. At the time cars were much simpler, much less reliable, and parts more visible than presently.

When my mother took the test in the Opal, she started driving around and was instructed to return and park.

"Aren't you going to have me back around the square?"

"No, anyone who can drive a car with that clutch knows how to drive. You pass."

The next day, the car was taken to have the clutch repaired.

Der Schwan and the Ferry

My father took my mother to, *Der Schwan*, a classy restaurant in Einbeck am Weser. (The restaurant still had its good reputation in tact in 1957, and it currently has a website.) During dinner he told her, "I went to the American consulate to inquire about sponsoring your immigration."

"Under what status?"
"As my wife."

To get to Der Schwan from Göttingen, they used a single operator ferry, probably a ferry driven by the river's current. They inquired when the ferry would close that evening. As it was their engagement night, they stayed at the restaurant until after the ferry was scheduled to shut down. So they returned to Göttingen by a longer route.

Sometime right after World War II, Dad visited Germany, I suspect as a consultant for Ballistics Research Laboratory, Aberdeen Proving Grounds. He met the ferry master, who scolded him, saying he had been kept up all night waiting for the two of them to return.

"Sorry," my father replied, probably in a manner that anyone who knew Joe Mayer would recognize as sheepish and contrite. "It was the night that my wife and I got engaged. When we chose to return, it was late, and we thought you were closed, so we took the long way."

About seventeen years of anger melted.

The Dinner

Following Der Schwan, of course there was a dinner at Maria's mother's house—where Joe was a boarder—to celebrate my parents' engagement. By mistake, it was scheduled on the maid's day off. There are somewhat different versions of the rest of the story. I choose the one I find most plausible.

Mother was in tears, helpless in the kitchen while my father was doing most of the cooking and some of the other work, such as setting the table. My father's response to my mother's helplessness was, "As expensive as maids are in the United States, I promise to hire one, ... as long as you remain a physicist!"

And Many Dinners to Come

Years later, on Thursday, a maid's day off in my parents' house, mother and dad would have cocktails.

"Peter," mother would say, "preheat the oven to 350 degrees, put the meatloaf in the oven, and set the timer for one hour. Be sure that the potatoes are around the meatloaf." When getting older, the instructions became less complete, "Put the string beans in the pressure cooker with a half cup of water. Heat the pressure cooker to cook and cook for two minutes—oh, by now you know the rest. The platter and serving bowl are not yet on the kitchen table."

Another night, "Broil the steak fourteen minutes on each side." My parents would purchase two-inch thick of thicker steaks. "Rub both sides of the steak with garlic if you like."

The responsibilities expanded and the instructions shrank over time.

Earlier, it was the same way for my older sister and for a while, on alternating Thursdays, with my sister and me. My mother saw to it that neither of her children would have her experience of being helpless in the kitchen!

The Wedding

In Germany, as in many other countries, only civil weddings have legal status. A church or other religious wedding is a frill. My parents accommodated the demands from their mothers—both my grandfathers were deceased when my parents married—and agreed to the inclusion of a religious wedding. However, the wedding must be held in the house, not in a church, and there must not be a sermon.

My father, with mother's agreement, stated that the civil ceremony was much more impressive and appropriate than a church wedding. It took place in a room in the *Rathaus*. My father described the ceremony as solemn and unemotional. The mood was set by the question, "Are you sure you want to take this major step in your life?" My father was awed by the old men in legal robes officiating. Men in religious robes would never have the same effect on my father. Mother described a mural wrapped around the wall, representing the stages in a person's life from birth through marriage to death.

An aunt of my mother was familiar with church law and knew a Lutheran wedding was not permitted for those who had not been christened. The idea that my father would require an emergency christening before the wedding produced considerable amusement. The minister asked my mother's aunt whether Joe had been christened. Her response was, "I suppose so."

No sermon! No such luck! My father recalled observing Alois, a ceramic lion cub, looking as skeptical as he felt. (Later, the cub to me had the benign look you would expect of Alois, the storied lion who was brought up by sheep and eventually married one named Shelastika.)

Aftermath

A relative of my mother named his son after Joe. In the German Lutheran church, the names for christening were limited to a list of saints. To the minister performing the christening of the son, this relative insisted that the name of his son's namesake was Joe and that Joe was a good American name. The minister asked if he was sure that Joe was not an abbreviation for Joseph.

"It is not. His name is Joe."

"Is it a Christian name?"

"Well, Joe was married in the Lutheran Church."

"The Scenery Is Still Beautiful"

Before the outbreak of World War II, the two would return to Germany. With the gradual establishment of a totalitarian regime, people may forget the implications of freedom, or at least of a free press. During an after-dinner conversation, in response to a statement, my father was asked, "How do you know?"

He replied, "There have been many articles on the subject in our newspapers."

The reaction was a skeptical. "But this makes Roosevelt look good."

There was a sigh of acknowledgement with my father's rejoinder, "Don't you remember when there was a free press in Germany? Roosevelt is not popular in the American press."

I learned much of the history of the march to disaster from stories about conversations between Maria and her mother.

After the rise of Hitler, Maria's answer to the question, "How do you like the new Germany?" was "The scenery is still beautiful." In one shop, the owner said, "Oh," and when the other customer left, he went from behind the counter to lock the door. He no longer used a formal title for my mother but used her childhood nickname,

"Tell me truthfully, Miesie, isn't it awful?" My mother's smile spoke volumes.

My letter accompanying the turning-in my draft card in protest over the Vietnam War contained something close to the following: "When a relative returned to her native Germany in the 1930s, her response to the question, 'How do you like the new Germany' was 'The scenery is still beautiful.' Our scenery is still beautiful, and furthermore the Civil Rights Revolution may produce the first society where distinct racial groups live with mutual respect and tolerance. The War has also hurt the progress of this revolution."

On her final trip to Germany, for Maria's mother's funeral, Maria returned without Joe. On the ship leaving Germany, Maria sang the Communist "International" out of rebellion, not praise.

Shipping Furniture

This vignette is included less as a story of my parents than as an illustration of national pettiness.

For some reason, not by request, my father in the late 1940s was on the mailing list of the Soviet Union embassy and some satellite embassies for glossy periodicals. After my father once said that it is sometimes interesting to see what they have to say, I would often look at these magazines.

In about 1950, the United States stopped the circulation of these magazines in response to restrictions in circulation of the US counterpart in the Soviet Union. My parents found this so silly, but then they recalled an incident involving Hitler's Germany and the United States. Hitler forbade the transfer of financial assets involved in bequests out of Germany. Therefore, much of my mother's inheritance was used to ship some of my grandparents' furniture to the United States. They would have shipped much less without the restriction on transfer of financial assets.

Sometime after this grandmother's death, an American judge forbade the transfer of bequeathed financial assets to Germany. His position was that he did not know the legality of his action, but he did not wish to allow such a transfer when Germany did not allow the reverse transfer. My parents found this action silly, but it turned out that Hitler's Germany stopped the ban on the transfer of bequeathed assets. Unfortunately, the ban on Soviet and satellite embassies mailing publications did not have the desired effect of lifting the ban on publications from the United States embassies.

Chapter 2:

GÖTTINGEN, AFTERWARDS

Silly Old Lady

While I was with my parents in Germany in 1950, there was a silly old lady to whom my mother demanded I be nice. My mother said she would later tell me why. She never did, and I now understand that my mother would not want me to know while there was a chance I would blurt out to the lady, "Is it true that ...?"

I made the connection at a dinner conversation in Chicago. Mother described a woman who was a silly old lady before the war and after, when I met her. As Maria put it, "She was the last person I thought would keep her eyes open and be aware of what was going on." When trains on the way to a concentration camp stopped at the city where she lived, the seemingly silly old lady took toys to the children on the train. She did all a person without position could do.

Yes, Mother, of course I should have been more than nice. The example set by this silly lady, who risked so much in a country with so little hope, led me to risk mere jail time in a country with so much hope—as represented by the very un-Nazi Civil Rights Movement—and with otherwise such freedom. I turned in my draft card during what I still consider an immoral and stupid military adventure, the Vietnam War. In my letter accompanying my draft card, I referred to this silly old lady as a relative. I was so disappointed when I learned that she was not.

Two Physicians

When my family moved to Chicago, my parents were treated by a physician who would not send bills. My father repeatedly requested billing. Finally, with his convincing sternness, my father wrote the physician, instructing him to bill or the family would find another physician. The reply came, "All right, in the future I will bill you my usual rate. I haven't been billing you because I know Maria Stein and Ruth Wichelhausen." He probably wrote no more. Maria Stein and Ruth Wichelhausen were two German physicians with Jewish ties whose immigration my parents sponsored. Maria Stein was half Jewish—enough for Hitler—and Ruth's husband was Jewish. My parents also sponsored Ruth Wichelhausen's husband.

Maria Stein would send me books for Christmas. From my wife, asking about a Christmas gift label in one of my books, we discovered that Maria Stein was also an old friend of hers. Following our renewed correspondence, she labeled herself as my oldest friend, which was true on two counts. Following our renewed correspondence, I paid last respects when she was ninety-six. At this time I learned that Maria Stein had accompanied the other Maria, my mother, during a school vacation to a conference attended by my grandfather.

My sister, along with family, lives close to a very good friend of Ruth Wichelhausen. Ruth would stay every Christmas with this friend, during which time my sister and family have enjoyed Ruth's company. Once, I had the pleasure of having dinner with Ruth. Joe and Maria's only granddaughter, Tania-Maria, on her sixteenth birthday, received a nice silver candy plate. The next birthday she received another. Upon receiving the third, the granddaughter asked wherefore the lovely plates. What is their meaning? Ruth Wichelhausen explained that Tania-Maria was the youngest generation of the family that sponsored her and her husband's immigration. She further explained that her husband's family had all been taken to concentration camps and that these plates were the only remaining possessions from his family. Now six of these plates are exhibited in Tania-Maria's home, with a silver pitcher inherited through the Marias.[1]

---

1. *Granddaughter of (Entropy)² , Tania Maria duBeau, personal communication.*

Family Education

During dinner, my sister discussed meeting a distant relative of Mother. In the conversation, my sister and I learned that Joe had paid for his education. Joe said that the relative insisted on treating the contribution as a loan and that, at the time of telling, Joe was happy about this. As Joe put it, "With the economic growth of postwar Germany, he has done very well, driving a Mercedes and so on."

Since my knowledge of the support for this relative was from a special circumstance, there may have been others whom my parents supported. No one will ever know.

Chapter 3:

ABERDEEN AND WAR STORIES

Background for Aberdeen Proving Ground and War Stories

In 1939, my father learned he was not going to receive tenure from Johns Hopkins University. Given this information, he sought positions elsewhere and accepted a position at Columbia University. The person responsible for Joe not receiving tenure was unlikable, so Joe was proud to steal his thunder. Before he was officially informed that he would not be receiving tenure, he told the chap that he had been granted an Associate Professorship, a tenured position, at Columbia University.[2]

As an aside, many years later, probably in the 1950s, Mother saw the gentleman across the room at a reception. She wanted to thank him, first for hiring Joe and second for wanting to fire him. The person, however, disappeared before Mother could talk to him.

During the US involvement in World War II, my father's principal work was with the Ballistics Research Laboratory at Aberdeen Proving Grounds in Maryland.[3] My father made the following statement about working on a nuclear bomb project: "I want to win this war, not the next." He later believed he was wrong. However, consider a problem I give economics students involving opportunity cost.

---

2. *Daughter of (Entropy)[2], Maria Anne Wentzel, personal communication.*
3. *Mentroll et al. 1985.*

Writing this story about a relative, I instruct, "Use the concept of opportunity cost to show why this relative might have been correct." Answer: the opportunity cost of (or in English, the value of) the talent used for developing the bomb is the talent's use for "conventional" weapons. With this talent used for conventional weapons, some of these weapons would have been developed earlier, maybe leading to an earlier completion of the war.

When assessing this possibility, remember there was also a war in Europe. To illustrate why my father may have been right, this section contains a story of the first use of a kind proximity fuse in Okinawa. Suppose some of the talent used for the bomb were used, instead, for developing the fuse. This might have resulted the weapon being available in Europe at Normandy along with being available in the Pacific during the taking of Saipan, Guam, and Iwo Jima.

(When more Pacific World War II veterans were alive, I would warn my students, "When I make this argument, Pacific veterans do not even listen to me and yell that I am too young to know anything. I do not dare speculate on their behavior towards you if you make the same suggestion.")

Part of my father's work included developing proximity fuses. Proximity fuses refers to any mechanism that allows shells with shrapnel to explode over the target rather than on impact, in other words, after burying themselves into the ground.

He made one trip to the Pacific theater as a civilian "weapons' expert." He was embarrassed that he never found an explanation for many of the things he saw and the lack of information limited his stories. I first learned about some details when he hoped I could explain them after my living on Guam.

As Joe put it, he was very busy and the people stationed at the locations, whom he would ask about things were also busy. Most of these people surely lacked my father's healthy curiosity. My Sister once commented in Chicago that the star constellation, Scorpio, is unimpressive. In the Northern temperate zone it is only seen lying along the Southern horizon and is not impressive. How many of the people my father asked about things would later remember "When Scorpio is higher in the sky and, therefore, brighter in the

South Pacific, it is a very impressive"? In Guam, Scorpio is the most impressive thing in the sky.

During the Korean War, Joe made a trip, similar to the World War II trip, to Korea.

Joseph E. Mayer, the Administrator

Joe Mayer rarely took administrative positions. When someone would inform my wife or me that a university catalog listed Joseph E. Mayer as Chairman of the Department of Chemistry, I knew he was satisfying an obligation by taking a rotating position. He was offered an administrative position at White Sands Missile Range. The salary was high enough that he could not reject it out-of-hand in the phone call giving the offer. Although he discussed the offer with his family, he had essentially decided to refuse the offer by the time he raised the issue at dinner.

It was fun for me and others to claim, over cocktails, and Joe never denied, that the following experience is why he never became a science administrator. It also may have been part of the reason.

A Dr. X at Aberdeen, when dealing with administrators, acted on his temper in an extreme way. My father was acting administrator while the person who held the administrative position was on leave. (I imagine the regular administrator was a military officer.) Dad was real proud that he had avoided a run-in with Dr. X, until one day. While the regular administrator was on Aberdeen Proving Grounds being debriefed, having not yet returned to his position, Dr. X came into Joe's office and he walked along a bookshelf and took each book in turn, throwing it at Joe. Joe said that Dr. X was so clumsy that he had no trouble dodging the books at the times it was necessary.

Good or Bad for American Science?

Was it good or bad for American Science that my father never became a science administrator? Although I pose the question, beyond stating that the answer is not trivial, I will not venture an answer. Of course, if Joe had become an administrator, American science would have lost a large part of his research and teaching.

As a project administrator, Joe would have been poor; his curiosity and understanding was too broad. Joe described the good project administrator as a person so narrowly focused on his project that he was convinced that it alone would win the war. Such an administrator would fight beyond reason for resources for his project.

As an administrator above the project level, however, Joe's breadth of knowledge and curiosity would have been a benefit. Further, consider the person described in these vignettes. Dad's direct, kind manner would have been an asset, as it was in Göttingen. He was not shy about exercising fairness. He correctly interpreted people's feelings more often than many of us.

As an administrator, he also might have benefited from his legendary temper, which also usually cooled immediately, unless the confrontation was planned. That is, he expressed his feelings verbally, but if his habit had been to throw books, he would have thrown only one. When he engaged in planned confrontations, he exuded sternness more than his anger. He had limited tolerance for nonsense—except as humor—and none when it involved bickering. When my sister and I bickered, we both were promptly sent to our rooms. I am familiar with a planned and extended confrontation Joe had simultaneously with my parents' maid and the caregiver for Joe's infirmed mother. Joe's mother had lived with my parents for over a year. Dad firmly and angrily demanded a stop to the bickering between them. My mother was afraid that both would quit, but both remained in their employment and the bickering stopped, or at least they hid it. When Joe believed he was wrong, he would show contrition and, if necessary, make a major effort to apologize. As an administrator with familiarity with people under his governance, I doubt his anger would often be misplaced.

Royal Blue—from New York to Maryland

My father would spend a three-day weekend in New Jersey with a day or two at Columbia University. I remember running down the stairs to greet him when he arrived. When going to Aberdeen, like others, he would board the Royal Blue train of the Baltimore and Ohio Line and take a Pullman bunk early in the evening, long before the train left the station. One time, two noisy women entered after many of the others had gone to bed. They kept gabbing despite being shushed by many passengers. In the morning on these trips, Dad always got up, washed, shaved, and dressed, finishing as the train entered the station. He made the Pullman porters uncomfortable, and they would try to hurry him. This time a colonel also was completing his morning chores as Dad was completing his. The Pullman porters were more concerned about the colonel since they knew dad's habits. The colonel was clearly waiting for Dad to leave.

As the train was slowing at the station, my father looked back and saw the colonel fill three paper cups with water and precariously carry them down the aisle as the train was slowing. He dumped the cups into the bunk with the two women.

This and That at Aberdeen Proving Grounds

I recall a few anecdotes about Joe's time at Aberdeen Proving Grounds during World War II.

Car Used for Commuting in Aberdeen

The following is about consumer decision-making under restricted availability, including rationing.

In Aberdeen, Joe kept an old square-shaped Dodge. I remember finding it old and funky when I saw it after the War with a vague memory of seeing it earlier. The car was a dirty grayish black. My parents' other car was a 1941 Ford. The Dodge, when they bought it, was probably for sale because it was a big car, which used lots of gas, and gasoline was rationed on a per-car basis. My mother said that, when seeing it for sale for eighty dollars, they had to buy it because it had four new tires, which were worth a hundred dollars. Furthermore, tires were difficult to find and sales were rationed. They sold the car for more in nominal terms after the war, and my mother was amazed that the new owners drove it from New Jersey to California.

Buzz Bomb versus V2

Dad was consulted to interpret intelligence about the German rockets. The information from spies contained inconsistencies. Perhaps only after the assault by the V1 rockets or buzz bombs, and the first use of the V2 rockets, did intelligence analysts realize that two rockets were being developed. As two rockets, not one, the intelligence fell into place.

A Sharpshooter and a Tank

A tank demonstration involved operating it while it was being assaulted by all sorts of ordinance. Unexpectedly, the tank stopped. A sharpshooter who had studied the tank before the demonstration shot a hole in the fuel tank with an infantry rifle. A vent on the front of the tank provided access for the bullet. Should the sharpshooter have been praised for finding and showing the weakness in design or criticized for delaying production by forcing a change in design?

One Proximity Fuse Story

One design for proximity fuses was to have the shells explode after a chosen number of rotations. (The term *rifle*, which characterizes all modern guns and canons, means that the bullet or shell spins around the direction of travel, maintaining the bullet's or shell's accuracy.) Shells of none of the venders satisfied specifications for time from launch to explosion. All, but shells from one prominent manufacturer, however, exploded at a consistent time after launch. The workmanship by all but this one manufactures was good. The error was that the proving ground design did not take into account that the speed of rotation of the shells decreases as the shells travel. Shells were accepted from all but this one manufacturer. The manufacturer with shoddy work challenged the rejection in the courts on the grounds that none of the accepted shipments met specifications. For a long time, our family did not buy any product from this manufacturer.

"But We Treat Dogs Better than You Treat Your Neighbor"

Two army recruits were arguing. A New Yorker said, "You southerners treat colored people like dogs."

"Yes, we treat Niggers like dogs, but we treat dogs better than you treat your neighbors."

I have told this story to blacks returning to the South, often after several generations, saying that I know one reason why they are returning.

With caution, my father said that the southerner may have been, rather than was, right, This reservoir southern civility played an important role in the South's overcoming Jim Crow and is behind positive response, without self-promotion, of southern whites to the Civil Rights Movement. For example, in the early sixties, southern white money rebuilt the black churches torched in Birmingham Alabama.

(I learned of white money rebuilding Birmingham's black churches form a black Southern Christian Leadership Council companion after an unpleasant confrontation with a Birmingham cop. My father observed that I was told this story so I would not be prejudiced against southern whites.)

Does Urban Life Corrupt?

When driving to work in Aberdeen, Joe would often give rides to people, mostly military recruits. He observed that rural youth were usually more courteous than urbanites, and that blacks tended to be more courteous than whites. Northern urbanites, when leaving the car, would often show no thanks and even slam the door. The northern urban blacks showed only a little more courtesy.

Officers' Observation Post

My father was an observer with officers shortly after establishing one of the Okinawa beachheads.

He Who Has Real War Stories Doesn't Tell Them

I doubt that my father had a real war story, but there is one I heard only once that involves grunts who did. He described watching a line of soldiers attempting to take a Japanese position and being beaten back. The next day, the line took the position.

I believe that it was in memory of the aftermath of this battle that caused my father to become stiff during dinner at Don the Beachcomber. As background music, "Taps," was played on Hawaiian guitars with sufficient flourish that I did not recognize the tune. My father became stiff and my mother asked, "That is 'Taps,' isn't it?" He recalled the playing of taps for the burial of dead soldiers in Okinawa.

My Father Loved Telling Non-Real War Stories

Many have heard the following story, from the same observation post,

A type of proximity fuse first used in Okinawa was made to explode with shrapnel over the target by way of a microwave pulse sent at a given interval after firing. These shells were not working; they exploded all along their trajectory. My father and others at the post learned that the proximity fuses were working correctly at the other beachhead. My father, making a point of denying credit to himself, claims that a colonel suggested, "I wonder if the radar on the ships is of the same frequency as the pulse for the shells." Indeed, that was the case.

Civilians and Prisoners of War

Official Japanese propaganda to her troops and civilians was that, upon capture, the Americans would torture and kill them. Like most effective propaganda, the claim of torture and murder had a large element of truth. However, there were also cases of exemplary and, better, even heroic behavior to protect prisoners and civilians. Nisei code-breakers would enter the enemy camp to persuade the Japanese to surrender rather than commit suicide. On Saipan, locals captured earlier in the war were given loudspeakers to plead in the local language for the local population not to commit suicide.

My Dad's assessment from the following stories was, if Americans can act as he described, so can any people. I fear that the accuracy of that assessment about Americans is only true about Americans at that time.

In Okinawa, to protect prisoners of war, an army unit was promised a case of whiskey for every live prisoner of war. The higher staff had to change the promise to a case for every prisoner of war who remained alive two days after capture. By that time, the prisoner was out of this unit's hands and would not be killed or seriously injured by them. The same unit entered into a village with tanks. When women, children, and old men tried escaping by climbing a cliff, the tanks blasted away at the cliff. (He once emphasized to me that he saw this happen.) He believed that a suicide bombing by a youth climbing on a tank with an explosive had provoked the action.

Don't Do That

In Okinawa, my father was doing archeological research on a battlefield; that is, he was investigating battle debris and collecting some to learn more about Japanese weapons. He heard a bang and a whistle pass by his head and looked up. He saw a flash in a cave, and again heard a bang and a whistle. He shouted, "Don't do that!" After the third shot, he decided to move, putting a boulder between him and the cave.

Guam

Joe came to Guam from Okinawa, sleeping on mailbags in a cargo plane. In the morning he got all spruced up to go to the office and discovered he was far enough behind the front that people celebrated Sundays. He went to a beach for a swim and to lie in a shade of a tree to rest. He looked up and decided that although he knew little about coconuts, it was unwise to leave his head under one.

Years later, on my first weekend on Guam, I took a break and walked on the University of Guam Marine Lab reef and took a swim.

When my boss learned of this, he mildly blanched and gave me a photocopy of an article from *The Guam Recorder*. The point for giving me the article was to show me that the reef is quite safe except for an ignoramus like I was at the time. Stonefish hide in the sand and have very venomous spines, and cone shells have a poisonous sting, some very toxic. Other animals with toxic spines were not included in the article.

When I sent the copy of the article to my father, he wrote, "Oh, I was told about some of these animals and about toxic sea serpents. I was very skeptical." There are sea serpents in the Pacific, although not on Guam. Sea serpents are very venomous.

Ulithi

My father and I were talking to three co-eds on the University of Guam campus. When they said they were from Ulithi, he responded, "I have been there."

"On what island?"

Although I did not know that Joe had been in Ulithi, I knew the answer. "In the middle." Ulithi is a beautiful large atoll; the fleet for the invasion of the Philippines assembled inside Ulithi.

He later told me that on one of the islands, there was a most impressive thatched building being used as a bar. The building was probably a men's house. Then I recalled the story about the bar. He had never described the building before. A large number of military men and Joe went ashore to the bar. They stood in line to exchange money for a chit. Then they stood in line with the chit to buy a drink. With drink in hand, drinking, they stood in line to buy a chit, and on it went. When it was time to return to the ship, they were too drunk to climb the Jacob's ladder to board the ship, so they boarded by being lifted in cargo nets. All but the officers, that is. Being lifted on deck by a cargo net was too undignified for an officer. The officers had a place on the island to sleep and climbed the Jacob's ladder the next morning.

Many years later, I met other Ulithi co-eds sitting at exactly the same place and I had to tell the story.

New Guinea

In New Guinea, native stevedores teetered while putting a heavy piece of cargo on their heads and ran with the cargo to the location where it was wanted. My father asked, "Are they working so hard because we are watching?"

"No, they always work this hard."

At another location, he asked, "Are these from a different tribe? They look different."

"No, they are women."

To defend my father, they might have also been from a different "tribe," or location. Often "one talk," or as New Guineans say to outsiders, "people from the same place," have a distinct appearance that is very different from other New Guineans.

These stevedores would work for three months and purchase western niceties such as radios and toilet seats. How they used these things, who knows?

Retaking of Corregidor and Gas Warfare

My father was present during the retaking of Corregidor, Philippines, by United States troops. The Japanese were in the tunnels, and the United States troops possessed the exits of the ventilation ducts. The United States was pouring lit gasoline down the ducts, which the Japanese extinguished with blankets. My father suggested using pentane gas instead. The hoses were already prepared to deliver the pentane down the ducts when the command received a message to ask the scientific advisor whether pentane is poisonous. Joe demurred. The message was repeated. Joe reluctantly stated that pentane, like all petroleum gasses, was somewhat poisonous. The responding message was, "Do not use."

Another part of the story: Although Americans built the underground labyrinth, the invading troops did not have the plans for the tunnels. The plans were top secret and locked up in Washington. Because of this experience, my father speculated, albeit skeptically, that the information on the nuclear bomb provided to the Soviets by Fuchs and other spies was in a safe in Stalin's office and never given to the scientists who could understand and use the material.

Notes on Korea

A few short items from Joe's Korean trip during the Korean War.

Night Air Reconnaissance

A means of night reconnaissance from a plane involved a flare, which lit after the parachute carrying it opened. The parachute shielded the observer's eyes and camera from the glare of the flare. The image from the camera just as the flare lit might catch soldiers with branches on their backs falling forward. Once they had fallen, the soldiers would look like bushes. It was a clever and simple technique of reconnaissance, but the Chinese managed to march undetected.

"Oh, They Are Much More Clever with Machinery than Americans"

Similar conversations were reported upon Joe's return from Korea:
"What are Koreans like?"
Joe's response: "Well, like Americans."
"Surely they are different from Americans."
"No, they are like Americans."
"There must be some way in which they differ from Americans."
"Oh, they are much cleverer with machinery than we are."
Laughter.
If you ever looked under the hood of a taxi in a third world country, you know what Joe meant and that he is correct.[4] When you live in the environment, however, you learn that most of these mechanics, although adept at improvisation, do not understand maintenance—that is, preventing the need for repairs and planning

---

4. *James Arnold, Professor Emeritus, University of California, San Diego, personal communication.*

for repairs. Examples of maintenance are changing oil and having an extra fan belt because fan belts break.

Japan Is Beautiful

My father did not find Korea attractive. The mountains were bare from people stripping all trees for firewood. The firewood in markets was tree branches. Later, I was able to inform him, that in South Korea, the mountains have become covered with forests. In his short time in Japan, he found the country beautiful.

Chapter 4:

MARIA'S TIME AT SARAH LAWRENCE COLLEGE

Maria and Sarah Lawrence

Joe accepted a position at Columbia University in 1939. In January 1941, Mother, after an association with Columbia, took a position with Sarah Lawrence College. Sarah Lawrence was a women's college. The faculty position was part time until the 1945–1946 contract, and she made it clear, "When my children are sick, I am sick." World War II interfered with an intended workload, allowing her significant time with her children. Although she was glad to fight Hitler, she regretted the extra demands on her time from joining the Manhattan (nuclear bomb) Project. In the letter dated February 7, 1944, during a year's leave, she stated that in comparison with teaching at Sarah Lawrence, "spending at least 40 hours a week in the laboratory is rather strenuous when combined with two children." (This has the sound of everyone's wartime understatement when it comes to personal sacrifices.) She worked first on Manhattan only, later commuting between New Jersey and Los Alamos, New Mexico. Initially, she was hired temporarily to teach one mathematics course to replace a teacher who suddenly resigned. Although all evaluations except one from her interview were positive, there was anxiety about hiring her, since her only previous teaching experience was with graduate students. The 1942–1943 catalogue had Mrs. Mayer instructing Introduction to Physics and Physical Chemistry. The latter was taught with Mr. Henry Miller. She also instructed mathematics the second semester.

In September 1943, Dr. Constance Warren, President of Sarah Lawrence College, received a letter from Harold C. Urey containing "I am writing this letter to request a leave of absence for Dr. Maria Mayer," it stated. "Dr. Mayer fits almost uniquely into the particular part of the program which we must carry out." At the time, Professor Urey was director of research for what we now know as a subproject of the Manhattan Project, separating the two isotopes of uranium.[5] So Sarah Lawrence missed her for a year, and she missed Sarah Lawrence. She returned for the 1944–1945 academic year and remained through December 1945, when the family moved to Chicago.

Since little is written in Maria Goeppert Mayer's biographies about her time teaching at Sarah Lawrence, this section goes beyond personal stories to include research of documents from the Sarah Lawrence archive.[6]

Sarah Lawrence College

Sarah Lawrence was established as a two-year college in 1926, principally as a feeder to Vassar. The first class was admitted in 1928, graduating in 1930. The College's first graduate was in 1929. In 1931, Sarah Lawrence was chartered as a four-year institution but maintained a two-year degree through 1946. My mother felt that the abolition of the two-year degree was a mistake.

"[A] central goal at the founding was to educate young ladies of good families to take their proper place in polite society. ... A centerpiece of the education was something called 'productive leisure,' an activity with which each student had to occupy herself for eight hours a week. Among the possible options: French conversation, modeling, art appreciation, crafts, make-up, athletics, music, tap

---

5. *The two isotopes of uranium, 235 and 238, are chemically identical, so they cannot be separated by ordinary chemical means. To make a nuclear explosion, one needs a concentration of 238.*

6. *Since writing, a student at Sarah Lawrence has written an excellent biography of my mother's time in Sarah Lawrence, framed in terms of the development of science teaching at the College [Jing Min Chia, 2010].*

dancing—and also natural dancing—observing stars, typewriting, shorthand, literary club, bird club, public speaking and gardening."[7]

Some of the options under "productive leisure" might be legitimate mainline college activities and others are valid vocational training. Never the less, the removal of the productive leisure requirement in the 1930s represented the early beginning of the shift away from finishing ornaments to developing thoughtful women. The 1942–1943 catalogue included a Psychology course, "Child Development in Our Culture," that seemed to contain legitimate college-level academic matter but also concerned how to raise children and get help for family problems. The fine arts section of the catalogues through 1943–1944 contained dance as recreation but not as a credit course. Through 1944–1945, the catalogues included Consumer Economics, a family-spending course. This was at a high level for a course with such a title. The first semester including finance and the second was general economics. The catalogues in 1942–1943 through 1945–1946, under The Natural Sciences and Mathematics, included the courses "Marriage and the Family" and "Marriage in Wartime." "Marriage and the Family" remained in the catalogues through the 1947–1948 academic year. From a conversation with an alumnus from the 1970s I learned that students at the time laughed at the school's original purpose: "To educate young ladies from good families to take their proper place in polite society." Current students (2006) are aware of, and amused by, this statement of purpose.

The hiring of my mother and the chemist instructor, Henry Miller, was part of the process of including academic intelligence in the finishing school's product.

I doubt that there is a firm date when Sarah Lawrence's transformed from a finishing school into a fine college.

Given the quality of the faculty and students, reflected in my mother's fond descriptions, there probably never was the intermediate step of a college. Kaplan [2005] in her history, *Becoming Sarah Lawrence*, represents the transformation from a school whose aim was "to educate young ladies of good families to take their

---

7. Kaplan 2005.

proper place in polite society" to the current Sarah Lawrence, which produces thinking adults, as a continuum.

She credits the influence of John Dewey, and his progressive movement in instruction, as a common thread running throughout the College's history. Two factors, however, likely were germane to the transformation: after having the same President since a year after its founding, the College appointed a new President in 1945, who served until 1959; and in 1946, Sarah Lawrence temporarily accepted male students under the GI bill.

The College became fully coeducational in 1968.

Maria as Part of Sarah Lawrence and Sarah Lawrence as Part of Maria

In a 1994 convention, I met a Sarah Lawrence professor. I told her, "My mother is ... and ..."

As an interruption she said, "Yes, and we know that she once instructed at Sarah Lawrence."

When dedicating a new science building in 1994, the College had Peter J. Price [1994], a theoretical physicist with IBM TJ Watson Research Center, prepare a biography of my mother. True, the acknowledgments and kind references from Sarah Lawrence concerning my mother after she earned the Prize could be bragging on the part of the College and not genuine memories; however, remembering Maria Goeppert Mayer as an instructor at Sarah Lawrence was necessary, to make the connection to the Maria Goeppert Mayer who appeared in the international news.

The following is from a letter dated November 8, 1963, from the President of Sarah Lawrence College.

Dear Mrs. Mayer:

I want to send you the congratulations of Sarah Lawrence College on your receiving a Nobel Prize. There was a spontaneous burst of applause in faculty meeting a few days ago when I spoke of it.

Many members of the faculty have spoken warmly to me of your time here. The College is of course honored that you number it among the places where you have made a contribution.

Sincerely,
Paul L. Ward

Her reply of November 21:

Dear President Ward:

Thank you for your kind expression of congratulations on behalf of Sarah Lawrence College.

It is extremely gratifying to be remembered by my friends and colleagues during this eventful and rewarding period of my life.

Sincerely,
Maria Goeppert Mayer

Proof that my mother was remembered at Sarah Lawrence between her resignation and her receipt of the Nobel Prize lies in one-third-page résumé for my mother in the Sarah Lawrence archives, dated May 31, 1950. No source was given for the résumé. A note on the carbon from the archives states, "Sent to Miss Constance Warren, at her request." Miss Warren was President Emeritus of Sarah Lawrence at the time and was President during most of my mother's tenure.

Correspondence to my mother included warm salutations and complementary closes—such as "My dear Mrs. Mayer," "Yours very truly," "Very sincerely yours," and "Very cordially yours"—that only partly reflect the more genteel writing of the 1940s compare with the beginning of the twenty-first century. The body of the letters include phrases such as "writing to express our appreciation of your work," "very happy about your work," "we are very eager to have you with us," "very happy" and "great pleasure" (in reference to my mother's acceptance of an offer), and "delighted to know you will be with us for the rest of this year."

Sarah Lawrence was asked to give my mother a year's leave of absence for the 1943–1944 academic year to perform war work.

Parts of an October 1943 letter reflecting Maria Mayer's feeling about instructing at Sarah Lawrence follow. The letter is addressed to Miss Constance Warren, President of Sarah Lawrence.

> I would have liked very much to have seen you and said au revoir to you personally, but it seems that this will have to be done by letter.
>
> It is very sad for me to interrupt my work at Sarah Lawrence, but I hope it is only temporary. The contact with the girls at the college has been very pleasant indeed and each year I have enjoyed my work more. Teaching and the things it brings with it, namely, the human contact with a group of eager and interested girls is a wonderful supplement to doing research work; all of which lead up to the fact that I hope to be back with you again.
>
> If told ... that if my leaving now imperiled the possibility of my return to Sarah Lawrence, the personal sacrifice demanded is too much and I would rather try and fight my draft ...
>
> All my inquiries around Columbia did not unearth any physicist, but I trust that [name of person] will prove to be reasonably satisfactory substitute. He is taking over a very bright and interested group of girls which I simply hate to give up!

The response included

> ... wish you all happiness in your work. I know how satisfying it must be to have such a feeling of making a direct contribution to the war need.
>
> I shall be very glad to register your desire to return another year with the Advisory Committee on Appointments. Your leave of absence this year will in no way affect the situation. Each person who is not on a three-year contract is reconsidered, as you know, at the end of each year and you will be reconsidered just as though you were here.

In February 1944, expressing her desire to return to teaching at Sarah Lawrence, my mother wrote,

> I would like to return to my work at Sarah Lawrence ... I have missed very much the teaching as it is done at Sarah Lawrence—not the mere imparting of knowledge, but the human content of developing personalities.

I believe that the importance she found in "the human content of developing personalities" reflected two aspects of her character: she chose to be more than a woman—that is, still a woman but more—and therefore could appreciate the finishing aspect of Sarah Lawrence, especially those finished products who were more than ornaments.

In the August 15, 1945, resignation letter my mother was extremely accommodating.

> My husband has accepted a professorship at the University of Chicago and expects to start there on February first ... In short, I would like to leave the College after the first semester. If, however, no suitable physicist can be found to take my position, I would be willing to stay 'til the end of the year.

> It appears to me to be inadvisable for the College to look for a "substitute" to fill out for just one semester ... I do hope that a satisfactory permanent successor for my position can be found.

> It might prove easier to find a physicist now, at the beginning of the year. In that case I would be glad to resign immediately.
> In view of today's news it should not prove too difficult for the College to receive the services of a competent physicist. May I make a few suggestions of names that occur to me? There is firstly

> Mrs. Charlotte Houtermans.

I include the name of Mrs. Charlotte Houtermans from her list, because she indeed replaced my mother. During subsequent visits to Sarah Lawrence, mother was thanked for suggesting Dr. Houtermans as her successor. Her letter concluded,

> The work at Sarah Lawrence has been very enjoyable and

interesting. I am very sorry indeed to leave, but I have no choice in the matter.

Very sincerely yours,
Maria Goeppert Mayer

The reply from the new President, Harold Taylor included, "In view of the fact that the students in choosing your courses have been choosing you, we would prefer to keep you with us at least for the first term."

Maria Goeppert Mayer's Physics Class

A review of the Sarah Lawrence course catalogues from 1942–1943 to 1945–1946 shows the evolution of the physics class of Mrs. Mayer—as she is listed as instructor of the course—to what Peter Price calls, "physics for poets" [1995]. The description in the 1942–1943 catalogue for Mrs. Mayer's Introduction to physics was straightforward: "A short introduction in mechanics, heat, and sound. The principal stress of the course is on physical optics, electricity, radioactivity, and transmutation of elements."

This early description, however, may show better than the later catalogues the substance behind the latter's reference to "science as a liberal art." If written by a less qualified instructor, the description might appear as a Mickey Mouse smattering from different sub-fields of physics. A clue to course's substance is the inclusion of what were, at the time, two frontier subjects, radioactivity and transmutation of elements. Although, as a single course, the depth of understanding in any sub-field would be limited, the understanding acquired would be firm and, to the extent possible, integrated with the other sub-fields. For example, the properties of light and sound would probably be integrated through a description of wave mechanics. The student would likely understand, at an intuitive level, the identity of the electrons of electricity and in orbitals around nuclei and in the beta particles of radioactivity.

Smattering science courses with lectures by prominent professionals can serve well for general education and as fine early professional courses. High school chemistry and physics courses, which do not have the benefit of prominent professional instructors, have to serve this function for the Caltech freshman, and for freshmen in science and engineering at other universities. At the college level, the possible quality of smattering courses was well demonstrated to me by three Caltech quarter-length sophomore general science courses. These courses covered geology, the types of biology researched at Caltech, and astronomy (the last of which I did not take). As far as general education, I still bore people and amuse myself by pointing to a formation and saying such things as, "Look! An intrusion! I did not expect such within a body of volcanic rock." I am sure that many of my mother's Sarah Lawrence students, even in their old age, still exhibit similar behavior. As far as a professional base, I took further courses in biology and geology, and the general science courses in the fields served my classmates and me well.

The description of the Mrs. Mayer's *Physics* in the 1943–1944 catalogue appears to have been written by the catalogue's editor (probably a good thing, since she was granted leave at the beginning of the academic year to work full time on the Manhattan, nuclear bomb, Project.)

The first glimpse of "physics for poets" is found in the 1944–1945 catalogue. The description of Mrs. Mayer's Fundamental Physical Science is as follows:

> The course presents man's knowledge of the universe and the atoms which compose it. It deals, consequently, with subjects which are basic to the sciences of astronomy, geology, chemistry and physics. Science is treated as a liberal art rather than pre-professional training. The course is, however, prerequisite for further work in either physics or chemistry. The laboratory work contains chemistry and physics as well as observation of stars. No previous preparation in mathematics or science is required.

The description in the 1945–1946 catalogue is extended, and the last paragraph explains the importance of a broad, integrated course as pre-professional training.

> The course presents man's knowledge of the universe and the atoms which compose it. It deals, consequently, with subjects which are basic to the science of physics, chemistry, astronomy,

and geology. The inter-relation between the sciences, especially between physics and chemistry, is stressed; the unity of physical science as a field of human knowledge is emphasized, rather than its arbitrary divisions.

The general student who approaches science as a liberal art will acquire a basic knowledge and understanding of the physical world and of the relation of science to modern life and thought.

For the student who intends to do further work in any of the sciences the course is especially important since it will not only present an introduction into his special field of endeavor, but also lays the ground work of the basic concepts of science which are needed for a thorough understanding of any one branch. Laboratory work deals with physics and chemistry and can be adapted to the special interest of the individual student. No preparation in science or mathematics is needed.

Note, the exact same course description remained for several years after my mother left Sarah Lawrence.

Occasionally, students would bring up the possibility of using the knowledge about radiation and the transmutation of elements to make weapons. My mother was mum when some students correctly speculated that she was working on developing such weapons. A major goal was for students to be able to understand news reports, far from a simple matter. Until the mid-1970s, science reporting was horrid, almost always uninformative or just plain wrong. The label "atom bomb" for a nuclear explosion illustrates the lack of science in science reporting. Mother was very pleased when she learned that, after the bombs on Hiroshima and Nagasaki in early August 1945, some of her students gave community lectures explaining the nature of the nuclear explosions. Given the science reporting at the time, these lectures were essential for most of the listeners' understanding.

The Sarah Lawrence *College Alumni* magazine [October 1945] implies that students were specifically prepared to understand the possible reports of a nuclear bomb.

Following the government's announcement of the new weapon,

descriptions of the potentialities of atomic power doubtless struck a familiar note to those students who heard Mrs. Mayer describe the role of science in post-war planning at a round-table held last spring. Hampered by the secrecy which necessarily surrounded the research, Mrs. Mayer nevertheless endeavored at the time to acquaint students with the bombshell that was to change *all* future plans of the world.

From the students' response to the news reports of the bomb, it might seem as though they had been primed specifically to understand that news rather than news involving physics in general. This, however, is unlikely. Her students would have been equally prepared to interpret news about a dramatic new sonic weapon.

Sarah Lawrence Experiments and Our Home

Although my mother was very much a theoretical physicist, her teaching at Sarah Lawrence included experiments to demonstrate scientific principles and properties. I regret that only during this writing, not while she was still alive, did I realize that a write-up of her collection of these experiments would be useful for teachers of science, especially to liberal arts students, for schoolteachers, and for others. She mentioned replacing fifteen amps fuses with twenty amps fuses. (Yes, I am aware that this is a fire marshal's nightmare.) She also said she used soap bubbles, in one case to combine the oxygen and hydrogen from water electrolysis. When contained by a soap bubble rather than something harder, the combination makes a benign explosion when lit.

She used one of her collection to demonstrate the existence of air pressure to my sister and me. Take a soft metal container with a lid with an effective seal. In our case, it was an empty container for turpentine with a screw lid. Put small amount water in the container with the lid off and heat water to boil, leaving it boiling long enough to have steam—water vapor—replace the air in the container. In our case, a stove was used; in a teaching lab a Bunsen burner would be used. Remove from heat—in other words, turn off the gas—and put on the lid securely enough to be sealed. The container implodes.

Thanks to my mother, as a science demonstration for school

and boy scouts, I electro-plated a dime with copper from a penny. I attached the penny to the positive electrode of a dry cell battery and the dime on the negative. (Once upon a time, there were dry cell batteries with knurled nuts to attach wires to the terminals. These dry cells were used for simple electric equipment, such as doorbells and lights for models of buildings, for school science experiments, and for children to play with low voltage electricity.) Both coins were put in the same beaker with a solution of copper sulfate. One could remove the copper plate on the dime by reversing the terminals for the coins.

My mother's interest in astronomy from teaching at Sarah Lawrence resulted in the family purchase of a three-inch reflector telescope, which gave many evenings of family education and entertainment. My earliest memory of my obnoxiousness showing-off was at a presentation on stars at a Unitarian Sunday school. I was about six years old. Most often, before anyone had a chance to respond to presenter's question, I blurted out the answer.

Chapter 5:

THE MANHATTAN (NUCLEAR BOMB) PROJECT

Fighting Hitler

Parallel to her life at Sarah Lawrence College, my mother was contributing to the war effort through work on the Manhattan (nuclear bomb) Project, first only on Manhattan and later on Manhattan and commuting between New Jersey and Los Alamos, New Mexico. After expressed misgivings at not being at Sarah Lawrence, she took leave to work full time on the project during the 1943–1944 academic year. Although she never expressed the feelings, I am sure she had misgivings that the use of the bomb to defeat Hitler would bring such destruction to her homeland. As an illustration of misgivings, I remember a family discussion with guests at a later time where Joe spoke of my parents finding it unfortunate that Schweinfurt, a town that they really loved, had to be bombed because of ball bearing factories. (Actually, I believe my parents' reaction was in response to misinformation for home consumption, that a bombing raid was unusual effective. In fact, plans for the raid were not followed, there was a large loss of planes, and half the bombs missed the target. However, there were many more successful raids on Schweinfurt.) Upon visiting Germany after the war, they were glad to learn that the ball bearing factory was in the valley and the medieval town above the valley was unharmed.

Her children knew that we were fighting Hitler, not Germany. She remained very German. This was reinforced after the war by a monthly family ritual of wrapping care packages for mother's friends and relatives. At worst, the statement, "We are fighting Hitler, not Germany," was a more accurate simplification than, "We are fighting Germany." In retrospect, it is the simplification that should be accepted now. For Hitler to scare us enough, we must recognize that Germany was the most civilized country in the first half of the twentieth century. Actually, this alone does not scare us enough.

Based on weak evidence, and knowing who my mother was, she knew that a similar statement would be appropriate for Japan. Germany and Japan differ, however. For Japan, a single person, Tojo, is less to blame than Japanese military leadership as a whole.

My mother let me know that Japanese immigrants and their descendents were not our enemies. My parents, along with their friends, showed displeasure with hysterical anti-Japanese sentiments by writing a letter to the editor of the *Baltimore Sun* in December 1941 or January 1942. The letter stated that out of patriotism, and to show proper hatred for our enemy, the flowering Japanese cherry trees in Washington DC should be cut down. Given the outraged responses at the idea of cutting down the beautiful trees, they were forced to write a follow-up letter explaining that the position was sarcasm. As Maria's son, I knew, before it was knowledge among my peers, of the heroism and quality of the Nisei 100th battalion and the 442 Regimental Combat Team.

My mother's work with the Manhattan Project resulted in good stories and the two of us sharing observations of one of my Caltech professors who worked at Los Alamos during the war.

Lobsters

During lunch, while working in Manhattan on the Manhattan Project, she would sometimes shop for dinner for her family or for items for herself. She became very annoyed that guards were required to inspect by put their hands through the packages that she carried out at the end of the day. She said, "I must shop for myself and family and I do not like people knowing what I purchased."

One noon, she purchased live lobsters for the family. Note that Atlantic lobsters have large and strong claws. Now, preparation for sale includes holding the claws shut by stout rubber bands. Previously, a wooden wedge held the claws shut. The wedge was put in a space on the back of the claw that closed when the claw opened. She removed the wedges and when leaving that afternoon, she demanded that the head of security inspect her packages. (My memory that she demanded that General Groves, head of the Manhattan Project, inspect the packages was childhood exaggeration.)

From that time on, the guards would say to her, "Mrs. Mayer, you may pass," without any inspection of her packages.

Living in Los Alamos

For her stays in Los Alamos, mother was first lodged in a women's dormitory. Prior to my mother's residence, a man took his horse into the dormitory to join in the fun. Therefore, there was a rule against male presence in the dorm. This resulted in combat boots being dropped on the floor at 5 a.m., since the security detail arrived at 6. Mother pleaded that men be allowed in the dorm so that she would not be awakened by dropping of combat boots at 5 a.m.

The reaction was "That's an awful place for you to live." She was given a two-bedroom house and, like most in Los Alamos, she had an Indian or Spanish maid clean once a week. ("Spanish" refers to Spanish speakers who were in New Mexico when the named changed from Nuevo Mexico.) Los Alamos was dusty. Maria said she could see her footprints if she entered the vacant room before the maid came. A Brit, who was collecting Navajo rugs for his return to Britain and—he claimed—kept them double on his floor, lent Mother rugs.

I recall two short remarks germane to her social life:

- Martinis were made with sherry due to the shortage of dry vermouth;
- When Klaus Fuchs was found to be a spy after the war, she and many others had the same after-the-fact reaction: Yes, Fuchs could be a spy since we did not really know him; one Englishman, who first learned that a physicist who graduated from Bristol University was a Soviet spy,

reacted with, "It must be Klaus Fuchs," again, because of a feeling that he did not know him.

After my freshman camp at Caltech, I wrote my mother that Richard Feynman was the most interesting person I had ever met. She responded with some stories about Los Alamos and said that, if I felt that way, I had excellent taste.

Intersection—War Stories and the Manhattan Project

My Father's Story

After traveling throughout the Western and Southern Pacific, Dad returned to Hawaii. He went to the post office and requested letters addressed to him, care of general delivery. That Dad had just returned from a long sojourn in the Pacific could be seen from his being unshaven and jaundiced from long use of an anti-malaria drug. Dad said he has never seen a man look more apologetic than the postal clerk when he said, "I returned a whole stack of letters two days ago with a note saying, 'Not Claimed.'"

So he made a person-to-person phone call to New Jersey.[8] The call was forwarded to Los Alamos, where the call was interrupted by security before significant conversation. My father, however, knowing that the family was safe in New Jersey and Mother was safe in New Mexico, stopped trying to phone Mother.

My Mother's Story

My mother, however, was frantic. Through a series of phone calls, she was able to talk to Joe. Before talking to Joe, the censor gave

---

8. *For those who do not recall when long distance calls were expensive and had to be placed through an operator--for a premium, one could make person-to-person rather than station-to-station calls. The intention was not to pay for the call if the person was not available and someone else answered the phone. A person-to-person call could also serve as a detective service. To find an individual, one could make a person-to-person call addressed to the person but using the phone number of someone like his father.*

instruction, "Be sure not to discuss troop movements," et cetera. Her reaction: "I haven't spoken to or seen my husband for over four months. Do you expect me to ask about troop movements?" She found that Joe was well. At the end of their conversation, Joe asked for her phone number. Maria was about to say, "PO Box 1663, Santa Fe, New Mexico, and try to persuade the operator that this box has a listed phone number" when the censor interrupted. Joe phoned New Jersey to get the number.

Note on PO Box 1663

Everything that occurred in Los Alamos during World War II was said to occur in Post Office Box 1663, Santa Fe. Babies were born there, as others died in the Post Office Box. Providing the Los Alamos phone number was contrary to security regulations, so one told the operator that one was phoning PO Box 1663, Santa Fe, New Mexico. Sometimes, with great effort, it was possible to persuade the operator that PO Box 1663 had a listed phone number. My mother did leave a phone number in New Jersey with our housekeeper, however.

Once, when others and I looked skeptically during a story about births and deaths in the box, my mother said that it was a very large post office box. Although I understood, I still have an image of an uncertain sized but large door with post office box combination lock. The door opens on a storeroom with fluorescent light and a light colored linoleum floor.

The White Sands Bomb

My mother wanted to witness the test bomb, but she was not in Los Alamos at the time. She arranged a code with someone so she could call Los Alamos and find the date of the test and go to Los Alamos to see it. During July 1945, however, security cut all phone communication in and out of Los Alamos. The belief—likely correct— was that the prospective event was too exciting for people to be silent. So she did not see the test.

In retrospect, or even from the point of view at the time, was strong security after the bomb's development desirable? If the Japanese knew that the United States possessed such a weapon and—very importantly—enough material to make more quickly, would Japan have sued for peace before the United States used it? Was there a way to let our enemies know, without exhibiting such sloppiness with security to make the information appear contrived and taken as misinformation by the Japanese recipients?

My mother kept a piece of fused sand from the White Sand's test in a cardboard jewelry box, as one might keep ring or a small broach. The fused sand was kept between two absorbent cotton pads, and the box was kept in a bigger jewelry box along with jewelry. At one party, while mother was showing the fused sand, I touched it. I could not understand why I was made to wash my hands thoroughly.

Our Dog's Name

Elements heavier than uranium have a larger atomic number, a larger number of protons or positive charged nuclides in the nucleus, as well as a larger atomic weight, the sum of all nuclides—protons and neutrons. These elements, at least on Earth, have to be manufactured. Based on—what turned out to be accurate—speculative theory, the isotope of weight 239 of the element with number 94 was believed, for weapon development, to be the most interesting of these elements. That is, it was believed to be useful for making nuclear explosions and was later used in the Nagasaki bomb. After initial manufacture, the element was named plutonium.

There was a fairly non-transparent code that scientists used to discuss elements; it was to give the last digit of the atomic number followed by the last digit of the atomic weight. The code was fairly non-transparent, except that the important isotope and the one most discussed had a number of 94 and a weight of 239. The code gave a readily understandable inverse of the atomic number, 49. Upon hearing forty-nine, my mother objected that the code was too simplistic to be of any use until a person tried using the code to discuss other isotopes.

Shortly after the war, we acquired a dog. Although my mother objected that the name Plutonium Forty-Nine belonged to a black dog, the abbreviated name, Pluto, stuck. I am the only one who remembers that his first dog license had the number 49.

Revelation and the End

One day while staying at Wauwinet, Nantucket, the family walked to Quidnet to meet with the landlord of previous summers—at least that was an excuse for the walk. While in her house, the former landlord said, "I suppose you've heard of the atomic bomb." (I do not remember this at all; I am sure that the conversation was meaningless to me.) As we didn't have a radio in our cottage and rarely received a newspaper, no, we had not. I suspect that this conversation took place August 6, 1945. It took place between the Hiroshima and Nagasaki bombings.

Making understanding difficult was that what became the "atomic bomb" was not an atomic explosion but a nuclear explosion. Heaven knows what an atomic bomb would be, although a conventional or molecular bomb could be called "atomic" with less strain on reality than calling a nuclear bomb, "atomic." My father's belief that work on the nuclear bomb would win the next war, not this, did not help.

The meaning was finally understood.

When returning to Wauwinet, my sister and I were required to walk ahead, out of earshot. I remember being tired and wanting to walk with my parents and being hurt that I was not allowed to. My sister, being six years older, seemed to have a general idea why we were required to walk out of earshot. At that time, my mother explained to my father the status of work at the Manhattan Project.

My parents borrowed a radio. This was the first of only a few times I remember them paying attention to a radio. They listened to news reports involving the war with Japan. The other times I recall my parents paying attention to the radio were during political conventions in 1952, 1956, and 1960, and during the Joseph McCarthy hearings. They paid less attention these times than in Nantucket.

Back to Nantucket: I recall my family being excited about something huge related to the War happening a second time. The news story five days later, Japanese surrender, I understood.

Some days after surrender, a Wauwinet theater, put in mothballs at the beginning of the War was reopened for an evening of amateur performances. I only recall laughing with the audience at funny sounds when a summer neighbor from Chicago, Mr. Adler, performed by sitting on a chair speaking incomprehensibly. (After the act, I asked my mother whether he was speaking German or some other language and my mother told me that the talk was meaningless.) My mother observed to Joe, correctly, that Mr. Adler must be Dr. Mortimer Adler. At the time, Mortimer Adler was a professor of philosophy at the University of Chicago. That Mr. Adler was from the University of Chicago was of interest, because Joe had accepted a position at University of Chicago commencing February 1, 1946.

Chapter 6:
JOE

American Instutute of Physics, Emilio Segre Visual Archives

Travel, Pre-Maria

Silver Mining

One summer while he was in high school, my father, along with other lads, took a car trip. In order to finance needed car repairs, they worked at a reopened silver mine. New technology enabled miners to squeeze more silver out of the mine. The workers were housed in tents in a valley below the mine. Three streets of the ghost town nearer the mine were refurbished. The lowest street contained whorehouses. The middle street contained poker parlors. In these parlors, the players sat at a big round table and the dealer, with a revolver as a sidearm, sat on a high stool above the table. (My father called a seven-foot diameter stout solid walnut dining room table, acquired with the late nineteenth century Chicago house and later moved to California, a poker table.) My father was sure the games were honest. The top street contained some homes of the foremen and administrators of the mine and churches.

After exploring the rest of the town, the lads decided to investigate one of the churches. People were rolling on the floor, shouting halleluiah, perhaps speaking in tongues, and shouting, "Jesus saved me!" "Jesus save me!" and other similar phrases. Shortly after entering, the preacher, or whoever was at the podium, pointed to one of them—my father says he is glad it was not at him—and shouted, "You there, you there, confess your sins!"

Joe, the Sugar Chemist

After graduating from high school, dad worked as a sugar chemist during a sugar beet harvesting campaign in Utah. I believe this involved routine assaying of beet juice samples.

He was a boarder in the house of a Mormon man's second widow. His fourth widow moved in with his second widow. My grandmother believed that Joe almost converted to Mormonism. This would have been true if Joe's refusal to believe in magic did not extend to disbelief in an activist God. He was impressed, however, with the decent social interaction and high morality induced by and associated with the Mormon religion. He emphasized that when the Mormons practiced polygyny, it was under a strict moral code. Earlier wives had to approve of any additional wives, and after the first wife the man had to show that he was able to support additional wives. Further, Mormon polygyny evolved in part to deal with a moral problem. The Church was particularly successful in converting Scandinavian women who, upon conversion, migrated to Utah. Unattached women in a frontier agricultural community have difficulty having a good life, or even surviving. Joe also enjoyed the Church-sponsored dances.

A problem developed when the second widow asked how Joe was going to pay for his board. The contract with the company included payment of board. He eventually spoke to a lawyer, who said it would not be a problem to win the case for nonpayment of board, although Joe might not receive full compensation. It would not be a problem, according to the lawyer, until he determined that the Mormon Church owned the company. No lawyer in Utah would take the case.

I have learned of more recent similar cases. A person with a large claim was able to hire a San Francisco lawyer. Unlike for a Utah lawyer, a threat to the practice of a San Francisco lawyer of a Mormon boycott is like a threat to an elephant of rape by a flea. One Mormon who was challenging a Church company with a San Francisco lawyer was asked how he could reconcile being a Mormon and challenging the Church in court. From his framework, his replied, expressing Joe's feelings, "The Mormon religion I learned from my mother is one thing; the Church organization is another." Joe's wording was closer to "The social interaction of Mormons and in the Mormon community was pleasant and moral; the church as an organization, however, was very corrupt."

Grandma's First Gray Hairs

Before his post-doctorate position in Göttingen, my father owned a motorcycle. Later, when a neighbor purchased a car but kept his motorcycle, the neighbor said that the motorcycle is so much sportier than a car. My father's response to my mother's skepticism was "It is. You did not know me when I had a motorcycle." I believe that he was glad that I was not interested in a motorcycle, since he rarely, if ever, talked to me about once owning one. I do not know how Joe felt about my riding on a bicycle on the roads around Chicago before and while in high school. My grandmother, who I cannot picture with hair other than white, claimed that she had acquired her first gray hairs when Joe bought the motorcycle.

Onion Soup

This probably took place after meeting Maria. He and another person took a wine trek, hiking down the Ruhr Valley. One evening, they arranged to stay at an inn, and when they asked where they could have dinner, they were told "across the river at the next town." When the two looked crestfallen, the owner said, "Well, I can give you onion soup." They agreed to have the soup, even though it sounded unsubstantial, and they were glad to discover that French onion soup is a hearty meal.

For one birthday dinner I requested a meal of onion soup as Joe learned to prepare by observation, and I have imitated his recipe when having onion soup parties.

Discussion of Paranormal Seemed Paranormal

One evening, Joe was pontificating to guests about possible supernatural explanations for independent but nearly identical ideas. How can people who have no connection make similar creations at the same time? About the only thing I could not imagine my father discussing is anything with a hint of the paranormal. I later determined why my father might be interested in this case from a story told by my sister.

Joe described uncannily similar poems published simultaneously by two poets. The subject matter was the same, and many of the couplet rhymes were identical. Joe liked that the two poets were more curious to find what had happened than angry or accusatory. It was found that the less prominent poet had published the poem earlier in an obscure magazine. The prominent poet sent a letter of congratulations but obviously had forgotten about it. Joe's conclusion was such paranormal phenomena were probably, in fact, unconscious plagiarism.

Why would a person who simply cannot accept or even dream of accepting the existence of magic—rather than sleight-of-hand—consider the proof or disproof of a set magical happenings a matter for discussion?

When asked for something at a conference, my father would ask the person to write. I believed that the reason was that the person needed the assistance he asked for but did not the need to burden my father with remembering something. He would put it, "he does not need the favor for me to remember." This was certainly a reason, but another reason was probably more important.

At a conference, a student was discussing his PhD project with Joe. My father did not understand what he was saying. About a month later, Joe was sitting at his desk and thought, "This is an interesting idea," and he wrote it up. The student's dissertation advisor phoned Joe and asked how Joe dared steal the idea from his student. Needless to say, Joe was deeply embarrassed and ashamed. Joe would ask people to write so he would be less likely to make the same mistake again.[9]

Joe's interest was not in the paranormal but in unintentional plagiarism, *his* unintentional plagiarism.

Wine and Prohibition

Baltimore Police

Maryland was one of two states never to ratify the Eighteenth Amendment to the Constitution, the Amendment that ushered in Prohibition. My parents heard that if you asked a Baltimore policeman where there was a restaurant that served wine, you would be informed. My parents tested this proposition. The policeman responded, "You asked where there is a restaurant. Down the street at the next corner in the building's basement there is a restaurant." When asking for wine in the restaurant, neither a verbal nor a nonverbal response was given but with dinner a teapot with two teacups appeared.

---

9. *Daughter of (Entropy)[2] , Maria Anne Wentzel, personal communication.*

Winemaking

For winemaking, my parents separated grape skin and seeds from the pulp and juice in their washing machine. For weeks after separating grape juice and pulp from the seeds and skin, the washerwoman was frustrated by purple spots on Joe's white shirts. (I suppose that before my memory, Joe wore nothing but white shirts. Surprisingly to those who knew Joe after the two moved to California in 1960, previous to the move, he nearly always wore white coarse cotton tailored shirts with two button-down flap pockets. He would have them made two dozen at a time. As far as I can remember, he always wore such shirts until my sister and I, with trepidation, purchased a summer sports shirt for Father's Day in 1956.)

During Prohibition, yeast was labeled with "Not for making alcoholic beverages." People who have more recently lived in Saudi Arabia are familiar with the ruse. So my parents purchased wine yeast in Germany and had it packaged with a label stating, "Not for making alcoholic beverages." Just adding wine yeast to the juice and pulp was wasteful, since the wild yeast would dominate the fermentation. Joe addressed the problem by sterilizing a quart of juice through heat and growing the wine yeast in this quart. Pouring this quart with a well-established wine yeast culture into the larger amount of juice and pulp would provide enough initial wine yeast so that this yeast would dominate the culture.

They found that the yeast defined the taste of the wine more than the grape.

When I asked Joe what vats he used and for suggestions on buying wine yeast, he recommended that I buy Gallo wine. "It is easier and tastes a little better." (Note: to an American, the Gallo brand epitomizes cheap wine.)

You Know, The *John Ford*

In the earlier days of commercial airline flights, sometimes liquor was available on the flight and sometimes not. My father would carry a silver flask with brandy. On one flight, he offered some brandy to the person next to him. The person put out his hand to shake my father's and said, "I am John Ford, you know, *The* John Ford."

"I am Joe Mayer, you know, *The* Joe Mayer," he replied. As Joe put it, "We were even." Joe was searching his memory of the Detroit Fords as a conversation similar to the following took place.

"Do you know who John Wayne is?"

"No."

"Have you heard of Clark Gable?"

"No."

"Have you heard of Olivia de Havilland?"

"No."

"Surely you have heard of Carey Grant."

"No."

"Betty Grable?"

"No."

This went on until: "Have you heard of Sonja Henie?"

At that point Joe understood but he would not admit it. "Sonja Henie. Oh, Sonja Henie's! Of course I know, and I have met Sonja Henie, herself. She owns and runs a Norwegian restaurant on Forty-Second Street in New York. Sonya Henie's has the best smorgasbord on Thursday evenings."

"If everyone were like you, Hollywood would go broke."

"If everyone were like I, Hollywood would have to make good movies."

Never Fly in a Lockheed L-188 Electra Turboprop

While waiting in an airport, a man sat down next to a gentleman near Joe and explained why he never flew in Lockheed Turboprop airplanes—because of the accidents this model plane had been involved in, et cetera.

Then the man sat down next to Joe and started to go through the whole spiel when Joe said the physical chemist equivalent of, "I am not sure if one has marginal cost pricing in this case. The concentration ratios are high, but there are negligible barriers to entry. Even the goodwill barrier is low, and the economies-of-scale barrier is nonexistent! However, it would take time before the entrant would acquire a significant market share, and the present value of short-term profits may be greater than the present value of maintaining the market share. Would all the firms agree that the present value of short-term profits is greater than the present value of maintaining market share?"

The man stood up, moved away, and watched Joe with trepidation until Joe left on his flight.

Ducks and Fish

In a train dining car, there was a conversation similar to the following between a gentlemen and my father.

My father said, "You look so glum."

"I am a poultry inspector."

"Is that a poor job?"

"No! It is a good job. I enjoy plucking the birds and poking the flesh to see if the flesh responds well, and I grade it accordingly."

"Then why are you so glum?"

"About a week ago I had a whole bunch of ducks from Oregon. I plucked them and poked their flesh. The flesh bounced back beautifully. I have never seen such fine ducks and certainly not so many fine ducks. I graded them all A1! You know what all those farmers in Oregon did? They fed the ducks fish, and now I have been getting complaints from across the country that the ducks taste like fish! Now you know why I am so glum."

Are You Afraid of Hummingbirds?

Perhaps the first addition to my parents' new California house was hummingbird feeders. As dusk was approaching, Joe would ask guests, "Are you afraid of humming birds?" Then he would take them to the feeders. My father would shine spotlights on the feeders to enhance hummingbird color.[10]

---

10. *Much of the color of hummingbirds is not from dyes or the color of feathers but the result of differential reflection. Some feathers have a thickness equal to a small number of light wavelengths—perhaps one wavelength or less. Light would reflect off both sides of the feather. Some light would reflect off the front surface and some would go through the feather and reflect off the back surface. As a result, the reflections for some light wavelengths are enhanced while others are canceled out. Different wavelengths of light produce*

As dusk approached, hummingbirds would swarm around the feeders. I doubt anyone was really afraid, but I found the hummingbirds disconcerting and if bumblebees acted this way, I am sure many would be afraid. They would dart from one stationary position to another—from, say, in front of a person to the right of the person's ear. (For a physicist, it was as if they were darting to different quantum states. This reference I will not try to explain.)

Memories for Fathers' Day not Found Elsewhere

The last conversation with my father included "You have been a good son."

"Yes, in the last years I have been a good son, but I have caused you a lot of trouble." When he demurred but remained speechless, I told him the response of a college friend of mine, whom he knew, gave to a similar comment about causing Joe a lot of trouble: "Have you looked at any other son, including your classmates at Caltech?"

"I was lucky to have had you for a father."

"I was lucky to have had you as a son."

I meant everything I said, except I doubt my friend's response to "but I caused Joe a lot of trouble." The phrase "I was lucky to have had you as a father" was an understatement!

During the same visit with Joe, I cleaned up after him following a bout of incontinence. I said nothing. I regret not telling him, "Although I do not enjoy seeing you incontinent, I hope your attitude is 'I cleaned up after Peter enough; it is about time he cleaned up after me!'"

While I was in high school, Joe would often drive me to school. It was capricious when he would drive me. Some mornings he was up early and drove me, and on some mornings he was not. We would pick up fellow students at bus stops. I remember an older student commenting on a physics problem and my father trying to explain the answer, moving his finger over the windshield as if drawing diagrams. (I believe that with a chalkboard—rather than

---

different colors. When seeing both reflections, the enhanced wavelengths or colors show.

using a windshield while driving—he could explain better than any high school physics teacher.) I asked the student to please not bring up such things while my father is driving. His driving while trying to explain the problem scared me. The student's response, "Yes, he was distracted from driving."

A story I would have loved more when I was in high school than when I heard it many years later comes from a chemistry classmate of Dad while the two were working on their PhD at University of California at Berkeley. At a party, this classmate was being made silly by the passions of a lovely female. This classmate remembers Joe saying firmly, "You're drunk and if you are not, say that you are!"

While I was in high school we discussed possible careers. I was interested in science, particularly biology. He very much encouraged my interest in biology, in part because he felt that the most interesting scientific work at the time was in biology. Furthermore, unlike new things he learned in his own field, he could explain to me the contents of biology lectures he had attended. Following a significant rise in my grades in my junior year in high school, he encouraged me to apply to Caltech.

I enjoyed cooking and was good at it. I would credit Dad for teaching me how to cook. I learned that anything good is better when cooked with wine. When I was a freshman in high school, he wrote me from Hong Kong: "I taught you that anything good is better cooked with wine. Well, ginger is a very good spice. It is used with a little sugar" (I now prefer honey). From this correspondence I learned to use ginger, especially when cooking duck or goose. Many years later I wrote, "You taught me that anything good is better cooked with wine and later you wrote about ginger. Well, anything good is even better with coconut milk." I then explained how coconut milk is squeezed from water and grated coconut.

Dad suggested that I consider becoming a chef. Cooking instruction in Chicago high schools was limited to "Foods" as part of the Home Economics curriculum. I might have acted on the suggestion if I had been surrounded with the culinary arts instruction currently available on Guam—the superb programs in the high schools, at the Community College, and at a restaurant that periodically provides instruction to children.

Currently, students in high school have expressed doubt to me about parental and other career advice provided by adults. As one student put it, "I am unsure if they are talking about what I should do or what they would like to do if they were my age." I tell them to listen closely to any advice that is out of character for the person giving it. I explained the significance of a suggestion from my Father, a University of Chicago professor, that I become a chef. (Cooking, woodworking, or home repair were natural hobbies for him; they were not natural professions.)

In a discussion about how customs agents can sense a person's dishonest answers by their look, he described how a British customs agent went through his baggage with a fine toothed comb after he was asked whether he had brought any gifts. He could not explain that the guilty look on his face was because he felt he *should have* brought gifts.

Some people excused a Professor Y for his arrogance and unpleasantness with "he is bright." My father responded, "No! He is a fairly good scientist, but this is only a small part of life." Most know this but many—particularly those with limited academic experience, but who hold the academic world in awe—do not believe this. This quote from Joe gives me an edge beyond my personal credentials. For example, when someone exclaims with bewilderment, "He has a PhD in physics, but he is so dumb," I responded, "I have a PhD in economics and my father has a University of California professorship in theoretical chemistry named after him. I know, as my father would put it, 'the ability to acquire a PhD in a particular field is but a small part of life.'"

Chapter 7:

MARIA

American Instutute of Physics, Emilio Segre Visual Archives

Congratulations on Passing the Abitur

When I graduated from high school, my mother told me she did not attend her graduation party because too many of her classmates had cheated.

She told another story when I had an onion soup party in her honor at Berkeley. In Germany, one receives a high school diploma, and to enter the university, one must pass the *Abitur*, which includes an oral exam. The Abitur is the rough equivalent of the American SAT exams. Because of what was available to girls in Germany at the time, the Abitur was not given at her school, so she and some classmates had to make a special provision to take the exam.

All the girls became quite worried when almost all the boys taking the exam at the time failed, until a man said, "You have no reason to worry. The boys are here because of personal omissions. You are here because of your school's omission." He then mentioned some very demanding theorem, which worried the girls. So Mother said, "There is a room with a blackboard. Let's go through the proof of this theorem." Indeed the oral exam included questions on the theorem.

During leave-taking, Professor Henry Rosovsky, who later had an even more impressive career at Harvard, congratulated her for passing the Abitur.

Maria the Snitch

Friedrich Göppert, Maria's Father

I believe when Mother was in high school, in her father's early death throes, Maria's father had a kind of fit where he was conscious but could not move, at least not in any way he wanted to. In bed, upon recovery from the initial fit, he said that he always felt that the men taking Jesus off the cross in a specific painting were carrying Jesus so awkwardly. He felt the same way about the people carrying him up the stairs to the bedroom.

Her father asked for pen and paper so he could write his will. Mother was of some help, and when her father started writing a list of small items that he wanted to give to specific cousins, nieces, and nephews, Mother said, "Nothing here is controversial or will be disputed. Please let me write the list."

Later, one time he took some medicine and said, "Look, Miesie, what I do with the medicine," and he poured it down the sink. Unlike when she brought him forbidden cigars, she said that she had to tell his physicians about what he did with the medicine. Their response was not to be concerned, "He probably knows what is wrong with him, while we don't." Autopsy showed a brain tumor so advanced that if found during an operation, the surgeons would have closed the wound and not attempted to complete the operation.

Maria the Road Bandit

In the summer of 1934 or 1935, Dad decided to take my mother on a car trip through the American West. I have given reference to this trip elsewhere. On the last leg, the night they would return home to Baltimore, they saw a restaurant with the marquee, "Steak Dinners, $1.29" (or whatever was a reasonable price at the time). They spent their last dollars on this dinner. Then they came to a toll bridge, toll 25 cents. Mother said, "Joe, step on it."

"In God We Trust" and "Liberty"

When my mother first came to the United States, she took a streetcar. At the time, the conductor collected fare by coming to the seated passengers and having them put the correct coin into a coin collection container with a slot designed to accept the correct coin only. In order to avoid having to determine which coin to insert, Mother gave the conductor a dollar of paper money. She was given change and was confronted with the coin collection container. When puzzled, she was told, "Ten cents." She looked at the coins and all she could find written on them were the phrases "In God we trust" and "Liberty." After considerable frustration on the part of the conductor and Maria, the conductor took the coin out of Mother's hand.

For those reading this in the United States, take some coins out of your pocket or purse, look at them, and skip the rest of this paragraph. For others, there are no numbers on US coins. In small script you'll find the words "one cent," "five cents," "one dime," "quarter dollar," and "half dollar," as appropriate. The last coin I have not seen in years, but it was common in earlier times. "Dime" is an American idiom for ten cents. There was no reason for my mother, although fluent in English, to know this idiom. To make matters more confusing, the order of the coins in increasing size is as follows: ten cents, one cent, five cents, twenty-five cents, and fifty cents.

Leading to inclusion of this story in this collection, a store, for the benefit of tourists, had taped under a glass-topped counter the four currently used coins in order of value, labeling them 1¢, 5¢, 10¢, and 25¢. (The principal market for tourists on Guam is Japan, and secondary markets are Taiwan and Korea.) I laughed at the sight with appreciation and in memory of my mother's story.

Maria, the Experimentalist

Mother was trained as a theoretical physicist, with little experience or training in any laboratory. (In a way, this is surprising, because her theory was closely centered on explaining or predicting specific experimental results.) Therefore, shortly after she received her doctorate, Joe recommended that she work for R. W. Wood (Robert Williams Wood). Later, Joe expressed misgivings about the recommendation.

R. W. Wood was the experimentalist's experimentalist. He did not receive his PhD from the University of Chicago because he had too little interest in certain theoretical issues to meet all requirements. Johns Hopkins hired him because, at the time, Johns Hopkins did not require credentials to recognize quality. (The Optical Society of America now has an annual prize named in R. W. Wood's honor.) The person, R. W. Wood, can be viewed in his collection of sketches, with commentary, *How to Tell the Birds from the Flowers*. Another view is a letter from President Roosevelt—the first, T. R.—expressing regrets that he was unable to view R. W. Wood's boomerang collection. Since, upon search, I have seen references but not descriptions in writing of his pranks, I will repeat family stories, making this a vignette about the lighter dinner table and cocktail conversation in the Mayer household.

While my mother was in his office, a graduate student came in with two highly polished metal disks, stuck together. Before the student started speaking, R. W. Wood set the fused disks with one disk down on the palm of his hand and let the student explain the problem. After the student was finished, R. W. Wood easily separated the disks. When the student asked how he did it, the response came, "You just have to know how." By warming only one disk with only the side on the palm of his hand, the expansion of this disk alone (and some warping) made the disks easy to separate.

R. W. Wood went to a costume party dressed as a devil with a live eel in his tail. Before or after the party, he stood on a street wearing the costume. Some young men cautiously and slowly approached him. As they got near, he spit into a puddle while throwing a piece of Sodium into the puddle. (Sodium bursts into a bright yellow flame in water.) The men hurriedly retreated.

R. W. Wood was staying in a boarding house in some European city. For this telling, the city is Vienna. He noticed that the day after a dinner containing a roast, or chops or other pieces of whole meet, the dinner included hash. After a dinner of chops, he put a nitrate salt that makes a very blue flame on the leftover chops on his plate. Sure enough, the next day, the dinner was hash. So while eating, R. W. Wood discussed the properties of the salt and its bright blue flame. Then he said he left some of the salt on his plate and held some of the hash in the flame of a table candle. Sure enough, a very blue flame resulted. R. W. Wood was evicted promptly.

After returning from Vienna, Bill Smith asked R. W. Wood whether he could recommend a place to stay in Vienna. "See if Frau von Greiner has a room and please tell her I sent you; she would like that." Bill Smith rented the room and just when staff was about to take his luggage to the room, he said, "Oh, by the way, R. W. Wood recommend this house to me." His luggage was immediately carried out to the street.

R. W. Wood listened to the bored guide who explained why the Emerald Pool, a pool associated with a hot spring in Yellowstone, is emerald color. After the guide and group left, R. W. Wood threw some copper sulfate on top of the spring. When the guide returned with the next group and started explaining, "You can begin to hear the spring gurgling now. The water looks emerald because ... My God! It has never been that color before!"[11]

Now, why Joe later expressed misgivings about recommending that Maria work for R. W. Wood.

My mother described R. W. Wood as the real "love and string and sealing wax" experimentalist. (I do not know if this was a standard expression or the creation of a physicist/song writer, Arthur Roberts, who worked on the Manhattan Project. One of his songs bemoaning and mocking experimental physics' evolution to the use of expensive equipment, the cyclotron in particular, contained the phrase "with love and string and sealing wax physics was kept alive.")

Mother was to measure the spectrum from burning sodium (it might have been another element). Everything was set up on a table in the middle of a room. R. W. Wood explained that you stick the grating on sealing wax here. (A grating is a piece of mirrored glass with closely spaced parallel lines etched on it. It disperses light much like a prism.) Then you put the tray with the sodium and spark source to light it here. Over there is the camera. Make sure that everything is lined up so that the camera records the spectrum.

Now that you are ready, you turn off the room light (this light switch was across the room), then open the camera shutter, then go around the table to close the switch for the spark that lights the sodium. After that, you close the shutter and turn on the room light. The film is ready to develop.

(Maybe it was following these instructions that Mother learned to swear in Höch Deutsch, or standard German, since the Plat

---

11 *Daughter of (Entropy)², Maria Anne Wentzel, personal communication.*

Deutsch vocabulary, to the amusement of some students hearing her, is substantially identical to Anglo-Saxon.)

She went to Joe, nearly in tears, asking, "What should I do?" Joe told her to have the shop make a light-tight box and put everything inside with the switches on the outside. R. W. Wood's reaction: "Maria, you are getting fancy, aren't you?" Mother, however, felt properly vindicated upon seeing the box being used many years later.

Mother carefully presented R. W. Wood with a table of the spectrum lines. R. W. Wood, apparently as a message of appreciation more than complaint, protested that he had to pay the journal for extra pages to publish with the table. Speculation reigned in the family whether R. W. Wood was really so distant from theory that he did not recognize a simple log relationship in the data or for some other reason published the tables.

The Faltböt Club

It was my mother who would tell this story. She found it easier than Joe to admit a subjective uneasiness.

A *Faltböt* is a collapsible kayak made by a German company and was a common river running and lazy paddling boat in Germany before (and after) World War II. There was a Faltböt club under the New Jersey side of the George Washington Bridge. (We lived in one of the many towns near the New Jersey side of the Bridge.) Before war was actually declared against Germany, my parents considered joining the club in order to have a place to launch their Faltböt. Then, in case war closed the Bridge, they could paddle to New York.

They just did not like the feel of the place and the people. Maria expressed a subjective uneasiness, although she mentioned seeing a swastika. The club was closed as soon as war was declared, because the facility was used for spying on shipping.

The Maniac

When I was growing up, I believed that the maniac and the ENIAC (Electronic Numerical Integrator and Computer) were two different machines, not one and the same. The ENIAC was the first digital computer. By today's standards it was a monster, weighing over 30 tons. Mother did some work with John von Neumann on the ENIAC. Some tales I have not found elsewhere follow.

To preserve vacuum tubes, one avoided turning the ENIAC off and on whenever possible. To keep the ENIAC occupied, John von Neumann had it calculate л to around two thousand digits. When the humans got bored with the exercise, John von Neumann had the ENIAC determine the degree of randomness of the digits—that is, measuring the relative frequency of the different digits. Near perfect randomness was found; that is, all digits seemed to have the same frequency. John von Neumann was but one person to dwell on why the digits of л should be perfectly random. Having the ENIAC continue calculating л for a few hundred more digits, however, and checking again, found the result an artifact of the particular number of digits of л calculated.

Some connections for the ENIAC were like those of an operator-controlled telephone switchboard. To connect a party making a phone call to the desired number, the operator would take the wire for the caller and insert its metal-capped end into a socket for the desired number. When the call was finished, the operator would disconnect the wire.

A difficult repair of the ENIAC would be required when the janitor would pull out a wire from its connection while cleaning the room and then replace the wire in the wrong hole. Needless to say, great effort was made to instruct the janitors not to replace in sockets wires that they accidentally pulled out while cleaning.

The ENIAC used IBM card input and output. IBM cards were about eight by three inches, with a small part of the upper left corner cut off. Rectangular holes on the card were used to communicate with the computer. Computers used card input well into the seventies. My most recent memory of seeing IBM cards is as airline tickets. Those with computer experience after 1954 are unfamiliar IBM card output and with the Maniac habit of chewing up IBM cards.

Spitballs and Edward Teller, Father of the Hydrogen Bomb

"Edward Teller, Maria, Joe"
CREDIT Photograph by Francis Simon, courtesy American
Institute of Physics, Emilio Segre Visual Archives

I include this story because it represents Edward Teller as more human than nearly anything you are likely to hear or read about him. True, I like his politics even less than those of his nemesis, Linus Pauling. The stories about Edward Teller are included in this place because my mother and Teller knew each other longer than my father and Teller.

When and before I was six, in Leonia, New Jersey, Edward Teller was a frequent houseguest. He lived in Chicago. I found it hard to believe, but it was true what my mother said, that my sister and I would see him less in Chicago.

He had a loud and exuberant laugh. He would play a game of spitballs with my sister and me. On the top page of a pad of paper, straight horizontal lines divided the paper into seven sections. Sections were labeled by the days of the week, in order from the bottom, starting with Monday. From below the pad we would flip spitballs up the pad. The spitballs were tiny wads of paper held together by spit. The smaller and rounder, the better. The scoring depended on the day the ball landed. Sunday, the day at the top of the pad, had a special score. Otherwise, I do not remember the scoring system. When we tried to play the game without Edward Teller, it was not fun.

A reporter from *Life* interviewed Mother extensively for an article about Edward Teller. She observed that her children say, "The Chicago Teller is different from the Leonia Teller." He was much less fun, but I still enjoyed him. The reporter asked about Teller having family in Budapest. Initially, my mother demurred. When the reporter persisted, my mother asked that this not be mentioned. Edward Teller provided some support to the family, and he did not want the authorities behind the Iron Curtain to make a connection between him and the family. Mother lent *Life* a picture of Edward Teller, taken in our Chicago yard pulling an African bow as if shooting an arrow.

To illustrate the depth of knowledge he would sometimes show, much later, shortly after the Israeli 1967 Six-Day War, I was entertained as an adjunct to my parents in his Berkeley home. Before Israel's attack, reports from Israel referred to a partial military mobilization. According to Edward Teller, a Los Angeles *Times* reporter by-passed the Israeli censors with the report, "The partial mobilization is Ivory pure." No longer do all Americans recognize the meaning; however, for years Ivory Soap would promote itself with it being "99 and 44/100% pure."

Baseball

Writing a dissertation is the last step for receiving a PhD degree. Before a University of Chicago PhD student in physics is accepted for writing a dissertation, the student was required to pass a written exam called the Basic. Later, an oral exam was also required. The Basic was a six-hour exam split into two parts. When there was a dispute among the faculty about the propriety of a problem, the question was given to Enrico Fermi to evaluate.[12]

For one question, mother's reaction was "I don't understand it. I could never solve this question!"

"Oh Maria, it is really very easy."

Well, Enrico Fermi also could not understand the question. For both my mother and Fermi, it probably was not the difficulty of the problem but its reference to baseball that prevented the two from understanding and solving it. So, University of Chicago physics PhDs were not required to understand baseball.

"Enrico Fermi and Maria"
CREDIT: American Institute of Physics Emilio Segre
Visual Archives, Goudsmit Collection

---

12. *I thank Son-in-Law of (Entropy)², Donat G. Wentzel, for providing the details about the Basic.*

The Two Marias

When I was seven we spent a large part of the summer in New Mexico. It was explained to me that not all American Indians lived in tepees, wore feathered bonnets, and were expert horsemen. This was so ingrained into me that I almost felt none of them lived in this manner.

Through an introduction of a common friend, we entered the house of the pottery maker, Maria Martinez of San Ildefonso. I was excited to see an actual American Indian up close, maybe meet her, and even go to her house. I have an image of looking up at my mother and the other Maria and my mother saying, "I always wanted to meet you since my name is Maria too" and both laughing nervously. I remember feeling and awkwardly expressing to myself that Maria the potter was more like my mother than any woman I had met.

After my mother died, I mentioned this observation to my sister, who responded, "I thought I was the only one who noticed the similarity." A biography of the pueblo potter confirms our observation.

Poles

Please, either read this vignette in its entirety or do not read another word. When and only when I am sure I have the time to tell the whole story, this may be my favorite tale about my mother.

Because Maria was an ethnic German born in Katowitz, which later became Katowice, Poland, during her United States naturalization hearing she was required to give up her allegiance to Poland. When her tongue was loosened, by either liquor or banter, she would revel in the pleasure she had in giving up allegiance to Poland and in raising the status of Polish immigrants at her naturalization hearing by her impeccable dress. She would complain about the city where she was born voting ninety percent to be German but becoming part of Poland.

After going around the world, she said, "I have now crossed the Oder-Neisse Line an even number of times." These rivers are the post–World War I demarcation between Poland and Germany.

Crossing an even number of times and being on the west side makes her more German and less Polish.

"What would happen, Mother, if I married a Pole?"

"It would be all right if she were from near Warsaw."

Maria would quietly admit that the countryside voted for Poland, which might have contributed to both her children making fun of her anti-Polish antics. (Until after World War I, the cities in Eastern Europe tended to be German while the countryside was Slavic.) Whatever the reason, I am sure that it was due to positive qualities in Maria, not in her children, that both her children made fun of her prejudice.

Years later, I learned from a phone conversation with my father that Maria was invited by Poland to a centennial celebration for Madam Curie. In response to my teasing that the invitation upset Mother, he said firmly, "Maria is very pleased with the invitation." A plausible report from this visit is that she sought to visit Katowice without success.

There was a reunion of Upper Silesian Germans. Upper Silesia contains Katowitz, or Katowice. The organizers asked whether she was the daughter of Dr. Friedrich Göppert, who treated them as children. If so, she was asked if she would attend the reunion. She attended but refused the offer to have her way paid. Her stated reasoning was that Upper Silesian Germans lost everything and she could not in good conscience accept payment from them. I am sure that there was a more important unstated reason, which I explain later.

After the reunion, when I visited home, almost the first words from Mother were, in excited happiness, "Peter! None at the meeting of Upper Silesian Germans were interested in returning Upper Silesia to Germany. The whole purpose of the reunion was to say, 'Hallo, how are you,' reminisce about old times, and see how the others were doing in their new life." In other words, it was like a class reunion. I am sure that an unstated and the most important reason Maria did not have the organizers pay her way was that she knew nothing about the organization and considered the possibility that the theme of the conference would be seeking the return of Upper Silesia to Germany. She would not want to be obligated to any group that wished the return of Upper Silesia to Germany. None at the conference were interested in returning Upper Silesia to Germany, except the American delegation, much to my mother's embarrassment. The American delegation wanted the return of Upper Silesia to be the focus of the conference.

Another Reform

A woman scientist was very upset over what had been written about her in a biography of another scientist. She made a special visit to our home to complain vociferously to my parents. An incident in the biography represented her as having real worry about the implications of the success of some of the work she had participated in relating to development of the nuclear bomb. Her worry as represented in the biography may have appeared girlish to some, but it was appropriate and was like her. (This part of the biography was eliminated in the second printing—good new-speak.) I found her reaction as silly and childish—not in a good way—and after the incident, I learned that my parents found her reaction to be overblown at best. I am surprised that they did not say so to the woman at the time. Perhaps my parents, also, were too astonished to react.

A woman economist wanted me to over-reference her and quote her inappropriately in an article I was completing. My response to her objection over how she had been included in the acknowledgments contained the following.

> While in high school I looked inquisitively at my mother upon a younger women physicist leaving the house. This younger physicist was unreasonably upset by how she was represented in another person's biography. My mother told me that she used to demand recognition and recognition on her terms. She stopped when she realized that all her demands did was to hurt her husband's career. I add that if she really acted like this other women, who I doubt, she also hurt her own career. Afterwards, I received all the recognition I could want.

When I demurred, mother responded, "I receive full recognition, not full pay." I remember looking up at her from the level of her thigh and thinking, "Really, Mom? Did you really ever act this way?" In high school, however, I towered over her.

Maria Göppert Mayer Strasse

The following is a slightly edited from a letter of thanks in May 1998, when I learned that University of Dortmund was naming a street after my mother.

> Pardon the delay in this letter of appreciation and my writing in English. My German mother did a better job of teaching my sister to speak German and did much better in teaching her to write German. Further, my German language skills have deteriorated by living in Asia and the Pacific since 1972, having the opportunity to speak German about once every three years.
>
> My family and I are very pleased to have a street, Maria Göppert Mayer Strasse, named after my mother. Some may not realized how much my mother remained a German academician through World War II—where, as far as she was concerned, "we are fighting Hitler, not Germany"—and through migration ending in the very un-German climate of Southern California. She carried the aura of Frau Professor as an earned title, not a title by accident of marriage. Like many in the United States with the aura, she struggled to be approachable, the American side of such people. I have been told that because of her warmth she succeeded better than most.
>
> Although I dispute the details of one of her biographers, we had candles on our Christmas tree that were lit Christmas and New Year's Eve. Yes, in our house as in Germany, Christmas Eve was the important day. Because of my mother, in Kobe's German bakeries in Japan, I recognized stollen and pfeffernüssen, enabling us to properly feast at Christmas time when living in Kobe.
>
> My mother and my father would both be very pleased with Maria Göppert Mayer Strasse. Except in the last years of her life when she began to fully recognize her accomplishments, she might have been embarrassed by the above comments on the name's appropriateness.

Gall Bladder and Lutheran

In 1943, my mother had her gall bladder removed. Before the operation, she had an argument with the physicians. As a result, after she recovered from the anesthesia, she was given her gall bladder and two dissecting knives. She found two sets of four stones. The set of larger stones she named after my sister and the set of smaller sized stones she named after me.

Much later, my father had such an operation. She told the physician of her operation and her inspection of her gall bladder. The physicians suggested she look at my father's gall bladder. We were concerned that he liked fatty food—he was generous with butter on his toast and enjoyed the fat around a steak—and that he would have to change his diet. His gall bladder had a big rock and a lot of gravel. Mother observed that it had not been functioning for a long time.

My mother, upon entering the hospital for her operation, by habit, put her religion as Lutheran. She was furious to be visited by a Lutheran minister who said from the pulpit that Harold Urey should be in church on Sunday instead of mowing his lawn. Harold C. Urey's Nobel Prize was just a small part of the person.

Ever since hearing this story in middle school, any time a medical or hospital form asks for my religion, I put down "Non-Christian Scientist. Few food taboos." When questioned, I say that all you need to know is that I accept the efficacy of medicine and that my dietary restrictions are not likely to cause the kitchen staff grief. I do not state my fear of a visit from a rigid holy man.

For many years, I have not seen the request to inform the clinic or hospital of one's religion and questions about dietary requirement are explicit. In my recent experience, hospital chaplain services have been with multi-denominational chaplain teams. The individual have usually been pleasant and certainly not bigoted. Working with a multi-denominational team necessitates a level of tolerance and interest far beyond the capacity of the minister who visited Mother.

Memories for Mothers' Day, not Found Elsewhere

Because it is so incongruous, I like to refer to my German mommy. I once asked a host who was speaking Cantonese with the waiter, "Please have the waiter bring chopsticks. I find chopsticks easier for cut-up food. I do not know why, but my German mommy taught me to use chopsticks." "I do not know why, but …" is my standard line when I ask for chopsticks. When in an East Asian environment, I add, "and I am glad she did." The host ordered chopsticks and said to the other guests, "His German mother was a Nobel Prize winner." Other times people who knew this about my German mommy let the phrase pass as a private joke.

Largely because of my mother's influence, when the family had Chinese takeout, we all ate with chopsticks for a while before retreating to forks. I remember her saying, "You may find chopsticks primitive, but the Chinese were using chopsticks when your ancestors were using their bare hands." I believe Maria taught us to use chopsticks because she wanted us to have basic social skills for all environments, especially in cultures she respected. Yes, a weakness for East Asian restaurants and living over half my life in East Asia and in what has been called America in Asia honed the basic skill taught by my German mommy. Never-the-less, I am glad she gave me the basic skill to hone. Furthermore, when camping, one can make crud chopsticks from branches when one forgets flatware.

Whenever dinner was served to guests in our house on a white tablecloth and red wine was served, she would spill a small amount of wine and without comment put salt on the stain. (Salt was said to prevent permanent staining from red wine.) It took me a long time to learn that the spillage was deliberate and to understand its purpose.

Although, as discussed elsewhere, my mother did not learn to cook as part of her upbringing, she did learn to use a sewing machine. She showed me some shoe bags she made when she was a girl. These included handmade buttonholes. She taught me how to use a sewing machine, and when borrowing a sewing machine from a person who knows who my mother is, I love to say that my mother taught me how to use one.

She recognized the relationship between the Cub Scout ranks and Kipling's *Jungle Book*. Since we only had a German translation in the house, she read it to me speaking English. (When she was younger, she would read French books to her father speaking German. Some of her language teachers were disappointed that she had chosen to study science at the university over languages.) My father would chuckle, however, with some of her un-Kipling expressions, such as, "The lion said, 'Damn it.'"

Maria had a Papagayo (an Arizona Indian tribe) basket filled with India head US five-cent pieces or nickels. One side of an Indian head nickel contains an American Indian in full headdress. When not living at home, I would collect these nickels and wrap them as a gift for my visit. She described these nickels as nonpolitical and so American with the Indian and buffalo on the sides.

I described my mother's discipline as "*usually* more subtle" than my Dad's. Mother's occasional spankings with a hair bush were laughable, preferred to my father's hand. Furthermore, my father's verbal criticism could be devastating. The "usually" is because sometimes she was, from her child's perspective, a big, tough, scary lady. When my sister or I would tell a story of a biddy, saying, "I will call the police" or making another threat, her response was "It is terrible to threaten to call the police and not do it." It was so clear that my mother would have preferred to have us driven home in a squad car than have us receive an empty threat. "Never make a threat unless you are prepared to keep it." Following her example, I add, "Never make a threat unless you have the means or power to keep it."

My first folding knife was given to me when my mother found it open. An open folding knife not in immediate use transformed the owner into a previous owner. As recently as a month ago, I received a pit in my stomach when I saw that I forgot to close a folding knife.

I have been asked explicitly and implicitly why I know that a particular woman's nastiness to another is because of jealousy—sometimes with an applied or explicit "How could you know when you are unsure of why she is jealous?" My explanation is "My mother taught us to recognize jealousy among US mainland

Caucasian women and I learned my lesson well." (Islanders express their jealousy differently.)

I sometimes say, "Believe it or not, my mother was a master of indirection." This is plausible for a reader of this collection but is hard to believe for many of my acquaintances. She never told me to send flowers to a host or a family or person who is nice; instead, she commented on how she appreciated receiving flowers. She would also leave garden flowers on my night table when I returned home from a long absence. Another payoff is that I accept, not just graciously but with joy, a gift of flowers. I married a lovely who, as is too unusual, gave her boyfriend flowers.

When it is clear, even to me, that my brutal directness will not work, I ask, "What would my mother do?" With my answer, upon occasions, I have affectively used the indirect approach.

My mother's favorite inscription on family Christmas cards was "Season's Greetings." She threatened to wait until June to send the cards and stamp them with a rubber stamp saying, "And a happy Fourth of July."

Chapter 8:
THE PRIZE

"Maria with King Gustaf VI"
CREDIT American Institute of Physics, Emilio Segre Visual Archives

Dad and the Prize

Many newspaper references to Enrico Fermi credit him with saying to my mother, "Is there spin-orbit coupling?" And with this remark, Maria Goeppert Mayer was able to complete the theory that led to her Nobel Prize. This is probably true, but there is also a contrary story.

As background, before the simultaneous discovery of my mother and Hans Jensen, magic numbers referred to the numbers of protons or neutrons that produced stable nuclei. Stable nuclei are difficult to change by fusion (combining with other nuclei) or fission (breaking apart). With the discovery—simultaneously with Hans Jensen—of an explanation for these stable nuclei, the numbers ceased being magic. The Nobel Prize was awarded fourteen years after their work was published. Awarding of the Prize long after the initial discovery resulted from their approach proving useful for solving other mysteries.

Mother talked to Enrico Fermi, saying that she had an explanation for the magic numbers and presented her explanation. Enrico Fermi's replied, "Maria, sleep on it!" Probably the next morning, a Saturday, she started to present her explanation to Joe. Before she finished, Dad—in this case his sternness combined with love—stood up and said, "You are right. I do not want to hear anymore. Go to your desk and write it up and let me see the first draft."

By the time mother presented her work the next week at a seminar, her thoughts apparently were way ahead of Dad's reading. A faculty member reported to me that he was surprised to hear Joe ask questions as though he had not seen or heard the material before.[13] The shell model was very much my mother's baby; however, because my father wrote very clearly, I suspect he had a role in the final draft sent to the journal. He stayed very much out of the way when she and the person who simultaneously developed the theory, Hans Jensen, wrote *Elementary Theory of Nuclear Shell Structure*.

Joan Dash in her two books [1973; 1991] reports that Joe had to push, harangue, and outright bully Maria to have her write the

---

13. *James Arnold, Professor of Chemistry, Emeritus, University of California, San Diego, personal communication.*

article describing the ideas. Although I can find minor details that are untrue, my sister reports that the softer description in *A Life of One's Own* [1973] is accurate and that my sister did peek through the door to see why our father was haranguing. As in *The Triumph of Discovery* [1991], my sister saw my mother sitting at the desk and my father putting a pencil in her hand to write. I know that my father had the patience and love to push, push, and push, in any way he felt necessary, so that a person could perform. He had the love and respect for my mother to push and harangue until he was exhausted and blue in the face. With this setting it in writing, Maria insured that the shell model was her baby, but my father was the midwife for what was initially a difficult delivery.

Effect of the Prize

I was a graduate student and teaching assistant at Berkeley when mother received the prize. An *Oakland Tribune* reporter interviewed me over the phone. He was the arrogant, boisterous reporter from a late forties movie; of course, he received little information after his inquiries about my girlfriends. While a photographer from *Berkeley Gazette* was taking photographs, I mentioned that I would have preferred learning that my mother had become healthy to discovering that she had received the Nobel Prize. This statement was quoted in the *Gazette*. I am glad that the national media did not pick this up. The photographer suggested that the Prize might make my mother healthier.

When I next saw my mother, shortly after the reward ceremony, the photographer suggestion proved true: the Prize did not cure her, but it did make her healthier. When I mentioned this to Mary Hendersen Hall, she pointed out that Joe had not noticed this effect. As Joe put it to me, "I see your mother all the time, and change is gradual; so I do not see big changes." Mary Hendersen Hall was writing a biography of my mother for *McCall's* and a longer one for *San Diego* magazine.

Before the Nobel Prize in 1963, my mother would make low-level complaints when receiving honors. Her words, "Joe deserves this honor as much as I. I am receiving this because I am a woman." This message weakened as she received honorary degrees in the early sixties. For the Nobel Prize, her statement was that the Prize was the top honor without the slightest reference to her gender. She ceased making any other references to gender with succeeding awards.

She remained unassuming unless there was a clear benefit to be otherwise. When a travel agent for a trip to New York suggested that he try to use mother's Nobel Prize to receive tickets from the New York Mayor's Office for a sold-out play, both my parents said, "Please do." (The Mayor is given complimentary tickets to major performances.)

Fur Coat

About two weeks after the actual awarding of the Nobel Prize, a man behind the counter in a dry cleaning shop discovered that I was Maria's son. After learning of the relationship, he related the following.

"Your mother is very unassuming. She was having a fur coat cleaned that she needed for a trip. The plant was having some trouble doing the job on time. She kept coming into the shop and saying that she needed the coat for a trip. I thought it was a trip to San Francisco. The day before she was leaving, she came in, and when it was not ready, she said, 'I am leaving tomorrow morning for Stockholm.' Then I realized which Mrs. Mayer she was.

'Sorry, Mrs. Mayer ... uh, uh ... Dr. Mayer or Professor Mayer! I have your address and you live on Mount Soledad ... uh, uh ... I will have it delivered tonight. Don't worry.' I called the plant and told them that I do not care how much overtime you have to pay. Have that fur coat ready tonight and deliver it to her home. This is for the Nobel Prize winner Mrs. Mayer, and she must have it before she leaves for Stockholm."

Chapter 9:

MEMORIAL

In Memoriam of my Father

For Dad's memorial service, I wrote two items, which are preserved and unavailable in an archaic electronic format. These were read by the Professor James Arnold, the master of ceremony for the service. The material, severely truncated by my memory, is presented below.

Joe the Father

It was often a delight to have Joe Mayer as a father.

While Joe was sitting in the living room after dinner, his granddaughter, Tania-Maria Wentzel, at about age two and a half, brought him a pad of paper and said, "Joe, doggie."

Joe drew a dog that looked like a dog, a giraffe that looked like a llama, a giraffe that looked like a giraffe, a zebra, and other animals.

When Marianne Simpson, at about age six, was watching a parakeet fly nervously into his cage, Joe explained to her that the parakeet was making a Riemannian transformation. From the point of view of the parakeet, the parakeet was outside cage, protected from the people inside the cage.

My mourning started when I last saw him. He was no longer

smarter than I and I could only discuss part of my excitement about new things I learned. Before I left, we had said most of the things we wanted to say to each other. He said, "I do not want to live forever, but I still enjoy some parties."

As Husband

One Saturday, Maria started to explain the insight that led to her Nobel Prize. Before she could finish, Joe said, "You are right. I do not want to hear any more. Go to your desk and write."

Maria's reaction to joining any organization was to ignore the invitation. Occasionally, Joe would say, "No, that one you should join."

In the last years, mother was disabled. Because of Joe's care, she was not crippled. He would hold her by the arm whenever the walking became uneven. My father could be patient in spite of nature.

Jim Arnold correctly disagreed with the previous sentence. He said Joe was a complex person, both patient and impatient. I described in a vignette, "Dad and the Prize," an example of both his patience and impatience.

Why Are You Here?

I gave the material to Jim Arnold about two months before the service. I thought of what I might add if I were to speak. I would have added something like the following.

Please, answer to yourself, "Why are you're here?" (Pause) About half the answers are "Because Joe Mayer was Joe Mayer, you jerk. You should know this better than anyone." For those who actually answered the question, there are probably as many answers as people. Perhaps none of you gave the answer, "because he was generous," but this plays a part of why all of you are here. Although most of the stories that follow are about both my parents' generosity, since Joe wrote the checks, I associate these with him.

We purchased shoes, or at least my shoes, from a Russian immigrant cobbler with a very small store. As I entered the store with both parents to buy shoes for me, the cobbler asked Joe to help him get his son tuition assistance as an entering freshman at the University of Chicago. (My silent reaction was that my father had nothing to do with undergraduates and undergraduate administration, so why trouble him?) While the cobbler and Joe were in intense discussion, my mother and I purchased shoes for me, being waited on by the cobbler's wife.

Probably a year later, I learned that the cobbler's son was a straight-A student at Hyde Park High School, and my father made phone calls to the admission office and saw that the son received a scholarship.

I would then have told two stories written in the "Göttingen Afterwards" section of this collection, "Two Physicians" and "Family Education."

REFERENCES AND ACKNOWLEDGMENTS

References

Chia, Jing Min (2010). *Maria Goeppert Mayer: Revisiting Science at Sarah Lawrence*. Paper for First Year Studies, Sarah Lawrence College.

Dash, Joan (1973). *A Life of One's Own*. New York: Harper and Row.

Dash, Joan (1991). *The Triumph of Discovery*. Englewood Cliffs: Julian Messner.

Kaplan, Barbara, Dean of Sarah Lawrence College (April 23, 2005) A*bout SLC: History*, Becoming Sarah Lawrence.

Mayer, Maria, and Hans Jensen (1955). *Elementary Theory of Nuclear Shell Structure. Hoboken*: John Wiley and Sons.

Montroll, Elliott W., Harold J. Raveché, and Jerald A. Devore (April 1984). *"Obituaries, Joseph E. Mayer" Physics Today*.

Price, Peter J. (1994). *"A Brief Biography of Maria Goeppert Mayer Written for the Inauguration of a Science Building at Sarah Lawrence College."* Source: archives of Sarah Lawrence. Dr. Price is an emeritus in physics research from the IBM TJ Watson Research Center. His familiarity with my mother at Sarah Lawrence stems in part from his wife being an emeritus from Sarah Lawrence.

SLC (October 1945). *"Faculty Member Discloses Role in Atomic Bomb Research"* Sarah Lawrence Alumni Magazine, Vol. 11, no. 1, 8–9.

Wood, Robert William (June 9, 2009). *How to Tell the Birds from the Flowers and Other Woodcuts.* Cornell University Digital Collection (currently available printing).

Acknowledgments

First, I thank the American Institute of Physics (AIP) for the photographs. Most are from the Emilio Segrè Visual Archives (ESVA) of the Institute. A colleague at Guam's Department of Commerce, James T. Hutcherson, liked my occasional tales about my parents. I would never have written this collection if he had not suggested it. Pam Eastlick of the University of Guam made helpful suggestions. I thank family for answering questions and for refinement, confirmations, and corrections. Specifically, I thank the daughter of (entropy)^2, my deceased sister, Maria Anne Wentzel, my brother-in-law, Donat G. Wentzel, and my niece, Tania Maria du Beau. I owe a large debt of gratitude to Abby Lester, head archivist of Sarah Lawrence College. I have many to thank for directly encouraging me or for encouraging me through their enjoyment of individual tales. An incomplete list includes John J. Cruz, Jr., Barbara Camacho Cruz, Bert Reyes Unpingco, John Urey, Jennifer Sablan, Kemm Farney, Dave L. Rogers, and, of course, my beloved wife, Mary M. Mayer.